DATE DUE

APR 2 0 1983			
GAYLORD			PRINTED IN U.S.A.

PATRIOTIC PIECES

FROM

THE GREAT WAR

COMPILED BY
EDNA D. JONES

GRANGER BOOK CO., INC.
Great Neck, N.Y.

First Published 1918
Reprinted 1978

International Standard Book No.
0-89609-068-X

Library of Congress No.
77-20396

PRINTED IN THE UNITED STATES OF AMERICA

CONTENTS

PAGE

A PRAYER IN KHAKI . . . . *Robert Garland* 7

SOLDIERS OF FREEDOM . . *Katherine Lee Bates* 8

MY SAILOR BOY . . . . *Viola Brothers Shore* 9

THE QUARTERMASTER CORPS . . . . . .

. . . *Sergeant Wm. C. Pryor, Q. M. C.* 10

IT IS WELL WITH THE CHILD . . . . . .

. . . . *Mrs. Schuyler Van Rensselaer* 12

THE PRESIDENT'S MESSAGE TO THE NATIONAL

ARMY 14

THE WORKERS . . . . . *Douglas Malloch* 15

BELLS OF FLANDERS . . . *Dominique Bonnaud* 17

THE DRUMS . . . . . . *Grif Alexander* 19

FOR FRANCE . . . . *Florence Earle Coates* 22

NEXT YEAR . . . . . *Margaret Widdemer* 23

THEN GIVE US WINGS . . . *Anthony Euwer* 24

IN FLANDERS FIELDS . . *Lt.-Col. John McCrae* 27

THE SERVICE FLAG . . . *William Herschell* 28

PEACE WITH A SWORD . . *Abbie Farwell Brown* 30

SQUARING OURSELVES . . . *James Montague* 32

THE WOUNDED SOLDIER IN THE CONVENT . .

. . . . *François Coppee* 34

HARVEST IN FLANDERS . . . *Louise Driscoll* 36

HAY FEVER 38

IN SAN FRANCISCO . . . . *Bernadine Hilty* 40

CONTENTS

PAGE

OUR YOUTH . . . . . *Arthur Hobson Quinn* 44

THE UNFURLING OF THE FLAG . . . . .

. . . . *Clara Endicott Sears* 46

MARCHING FORTH TO WAR 48

THE SPIRIT OF '17 . . . *Mary Herrick Smith* 50

IN WARTIME . . *Mrs. Schuyler Van Rensselaer* 55

THE MISCREANT . . . *Dr. Felix E. Schelling* 56

THE LITTLE ONE-STAR FLAG . . *Damon Runyon* 59

RISE UP! RISE UP, CRUSADERS! . . . . .

. . . . *Edward Van Zile* 61

JUST THINKING . . . . *Hudson Hawley* 64

THE STARS . . . . *Agnes McConnell Sligh* 66

MY SON . . . . . *Dr. James D. Hughes* 67

SALUTATORY . . . *Angele Maraval-Berthoin* 70

ONLY A VOLUNTEER, *Corporal Richard D. Irwin* 72

THE SAILOR-MAN . . . *M. A. DeWolf Howe* 73

THE COST . . . . *Ethel Lloyd Patterson* 75

THE EYES OF WAR . . . . . . *Chart Pitt* 78

FILE THREE 79

THE SOLDIER . . . . *Christopher Morley* 80

OUR GIFT . . . . . . *Caroline Ticknor* 81

ASLEEP BY THE IRISH SEA . . . .

. . . . . *Elizabeth Glendenning Ring* 82

COLUMBIA COMES . . *Thomas Meek Butler* 83

A NATION'S PRAYER FOR STRENGTH TO SERVE . 84

OLD GLORY . . . . . *George B. Hynson* 87

SCREENS . . . . *W. M. Letts* 88

EFFICIENCY . . . . *Dr. Felix E. Schelling* 89

SEVEN DAYS' LEAVE . . . *Captain Blackall* 92

THE STAR SPANGLED BANNER—WITH VARIATIONS 93

ON TO VICTORY! . . . *Theodore Roosevelt* 95

CONTENTS

		PAGE
MIZPAH	*Gertrude Stewart*	98
THE FLAG	*Dr. Felix E. Schelling*	100
"HONEY" DRAWS THE LINE		101
MARY	*Irene McLeod*	102
PRESIDENT WILSON'S FLAG DAY ADDRESS		106
THE BELGIAN FLAG	*E. Cammaerts*	110
FLY A CLEAN FLAG	*Edgar A. Guest*	112
THE OLD ROAD TO PARADISE,	*Margaret Widdemer*	114
AS THEY LEAVE US	*Florence Earle Coates*	116
"WE ARE OF ONE BLOOD,"	*Rev. C. L. McIrvine*	118
THE TRUMPET CALL	*Caroline Ticknor*	121
THE MAN WHO CAN FIGHT AND SMILE		
	Norma Bright Carson	124
MAKERS OF THE FLAG	*Franklin K. Lane*	125
FATHER AND SON	*Calvin Dill Wilson*	129
THE PARADE	*Minna Irving*	132
THE NIGHTINGALES OF FLANDERS		
	Grace Hazard Conkling	133
TO FRANCE	*Edwin Curran*	134
LANGEMARCK AT YPRES	*Wilfred Campbell*	136
WHAT IS PATRIOTISM?	*Agnes Repplier*	141
THE WRIST WATCH MAN	*Edgar A. Guest*	146
GOD SPEED OUR SOLDIERS	*George Frederic Viett*	148
FORGET IT, SOLDIER!	*C. F. R.*	149
LA BASSÉE ROAD	*Patrick MacGill*	151
THE NEW BANNER	*Katrina Trask*	153
THE COMB BAND	*Berton Braley*	155
TO THE GLORY OF THE NEEDLE		157
FIRST U. S. SOLDIER DEAD BURIED IN FRANCE		159
THE HUN WITH THE GUN	*Will P. Snyder*	161
OUT OF FLANDERS	*James Norman Hall*	162

CONTENTS

PAGE

NO MAN'S LAND . . . . . . J. Knight-Adkin 165

IN SERVICE . . . . J. E. Evans 167

THE AMERICAN . . . . Hawthorne Daniel 169

CONSOLATION 177

OFF DUTY . . . . Patrick MacGill 179

LITTLE MOTHER . . . Everard Jack Appleton 181

THE MOTHER ON THE SIDEWALK, Edgar A. Guest 183

SINCE YOU WENT AWAY . . . Allison Brown 185

MARCHING AWAY . . . . Emma A. E. Lente 187

THE PRAYER . . . . Amelia Josephine Burr 189

ON ACTIVE SERVICE . . . Patrick MacGill 192

THE AMERICANS COME! . Elizabeth A. Wilbur 194

TO A CANADIAN AVIATOR WHO DIED FOR HIS
  COUNTRY IN FRANCE, Ducan Campbell Scott 195

AMERICA GOES IN SINGING 197

THE KID HAS GONE TO THE COLORS . . . .
  . . . . William Herschell 200

RHEIMS . . . . . Margaret Steele Anderson 202

MATEY . . . . Patrick MacGill 205

THE OHIO MEN . . . . . . Edwin Curran 206

A CAROL FROM FLANDERS . . Frederick Niven 208

THE RIDERS . . . . . Herman Hagedorn 210

THE CONVERSATION BOOK 214

THE SOLDIER'S MOTHER 216

IN PRAISE OF RIGHTEOUS WAR . Walter Malone 218

YOUR LAD AND MY LAD . . Randall Parrish 221

BOTH WORSHIPPED THE SAME GREAT NAME . . 223

PATRIOTIC PIECES
FROM
THE GREAT WAR

A PRAYER IN KHAKI

Permission of The Outlook Company, New York City

O LORD, my God, accept my prayer of
thanks
That Thou hast placed me humbly in
the ranks
Where I can do my part, all unafraid —
A simple soldier in Thy great crusade.

I pray thee, Lord, let others take command;
Enough for me, a rifle in my hand,.
Thy blood-red banner ever leading me
Where I can fight for liberty and Thee.

Give others, God, the glory; mine the right
To stand beside my comrades in the fight,
To die, if need be, in some foreign land —
Absolved and solaced by a soldier's hand.

O Lord, my God, pray harken to my prayer
And keep me ever humble, keep me where
The fight is thickest, where, 'midst steel and
flame,
Thy sons give battle, calling on Thy name.

— ROBERT GARLAND

SOLDIERS OF FREEDOM

By permission of the author

They veiled their souls with laughter
  And many a mocking pose,
These lads who follow after
  Wherever Freedom goes;
These lads we used to censure
  For levity and ease
On Freedom's high adventure
  Go shining overseas.

Our springing tears adore them
  These boys at school and play,
Fair-fortuned years before them,
  Alas! but yesterday.
Divine with sudden splendor
  — Oh how our eyes were blind! —
In careless self-surrender
  They battle for mankind.

Soldiers of Freedom!   Gleaming
  And golden they depart,
Transfigured by the dreaming
  Of boyhood's hidden heart.
Her lovers they confess them
  And, rushing on her foes,
Toss her their youth — God bless them! —
  As lightly as a rose.

                    — KATHARINE LEE BATES

MY SAILOR BOY

Used by permission of the author

I did not ask for strength to let him go
   (Although he seemed so young — still but a
     child) ;
I did not pray for courage — God, you know —
   When down the silver street, blue clad, they
     filed.
More than my life went with them through the
     snow,
   And yet, dear God — you saw — I smiled —
     I smiled.

But oh! how shall I pass each day his door
   Where still the shadow of his presence lin-
     gers?
How touch the things he loved to touch,
   Still warm and vibrant from his dear brown
     fingers?
How tread the silent floors his glad feet trod,
   Day after day — unless you help me — God!
            — VIOLA BROTHERS SHORE

THE QUARTERMASTER CORPS

The Quartermaster Corps
Is a non-combatin' crowd,
An' it isn't much excitin'
Fer th' man who likes it loud;
But it's got its own hard work t' do,
An' they'd all be on th' floor
If it wasn't for the non-combatin'
Quartermaster Corps.

The Quartermaster Corps
Sheds no glory or renown,
But it's got the grub that keeps you
Comin' back when you are down;
An' the Infantree an' Cavalree
Would all be on the floor
If it wasn't fer the non-combatin'
Quartermaster Corps.

The Quartermaster Corps
Is ol' Jimmy-on-the-Spot
When it comes to gettin' chow
To th' line where things are hot;
Why, the boys up in the trenches
Would all be on the floor
If it wasn't fer the non-combatin'
Quartermaster Corps.

The Quartermaster Corps
Don't use bayonets or guns,
But they do a mighty lot o' work
To help clean up th' Huns;
So here's something to remember —
You might all be on the floor
If it wasn't fer the non-combatin'
Quartermaster Corps!

    — WILLIAM C. PRYOR, SGT., Q.M.C.

IT IS WELL WITH THE CHILD

By permission of the author and the publishers, the *Atlantic Monthly Company,* Boston

The word has come — On the field of battle,
　　dead.
Sorrow is mine but there is no more dread.

I am his mother.   See, I do not say,
' I was; ' he is, not was, my son.   Today
He rests, is safe, is well; he is at ease
From pain, cold, thirst, and fever of disease,
And horror of red tasks undone or done.
Now he has dropped the load he bore, my son,
And now my heart is lightened of all fears,
Sorrow is mine and streams of lonely tears,
But not too heavy for the carrying is
The burden that is only mine, not his.

At eventide I may lay down my head,
Not wondering upon what dreadful bed
Perchance — nay, all but certainly — he lies;
And with the morn I may in turn arise,
Glad of the light, of sleep, of food, now he
Is where sweet waters and green meadows be
And golden apples.   How it was he died
I know not, but my heart is satisfied:
Never again of all my days shall one
Bring anguish for the anguish of my son.

Sorrow is mine but there is no more dread.
The word has come — On the field of battle,
  dead.

      — MRS. SCHUYLER VAN RENSSELAER

THE PRESIDENT'S MESSAGE TO THE NATIONAL ARMY

Washington, D. C., September 3, 1917

To the Soldiers of the National Army:

You are undertaking a great duty. The heart of the whole country is with you.

Everything that you do will be watched with the deepest interest and with the deepest solicitude, not only by those who are near and dear to you, but by the whole nation besides. For this great war draws us all together, makes us all comrades and brothers, as all true Americans felt themselves to be when we first made good our national independence.

The eyes of all the world will be upon you, because you are in some special sense the soldiers of freedom. Let it be your pride, therefore, to show all men everywhere not only what good soldiers you are, but also what good men you are, keeping yourselves fit and straight in everything and pure and clean through and through.

Let us set for ourselves a standard so high that it will be a glory to live up to, and then let us live up to it and add a new laurel to the crown of America.

My affectionate confidence goes with you in every battle, and every test. God keep and guide you!
— WOODROW WILSON

THE WORKERS

By permission of the author

We laid the keel of the ship that sails the waters
of peace or war.
We built her strong for the strongest gales, and
big for the load she bore!
We made the ship and we made her great with
the things that we put inside —
We made the ship and we made the freight, the
seas of the world to ride!

If a ship of war, then we made her guns — if a
ship of trade, her wares!
She's built of the bone of the working ones, and
the blood of her flag is theirs!
Sailor or soldier or citizen she will carry across
the main —
She's made of the muscle of working men, and
born of the worker's brain.

The load of her deck, the grain of her hold,
whatever her cargo be,
Food or clothing or goods or gold, whatever
she takes to sea,
The sower's arm or the toiler's toil made ready
the thing to go —
The shop's machine or the farmer's soil or the
forge's lusty blow!

The birds of the sea must nest on land, on the
    land the birds are born;
They must take their stores from the toiler's
    hand, they must take their wheat and corn;
For they who sail are a mighty race, and serv-
    ing a mighty need —
But he who stands in the Worker's place is serv-
    ing the world indeed!

                         — Douglas Malloch

BELLS OF FLANDERS

Sunday it is in Flanders,
    And, blue as flax, the sky
O'er plain and windmill stretches
    Its peaceful canopy.
The bells, high in the belfries,
    Are singing blithe and gay,
The overflowing gladness
    Of coming Holiday.
        Ring out!   Ring on!   Ring loudly
          The merry Flemish peal!

But suddenly there rises
    To heaven a cry of fear —
Quick!   To the belfry, quickly!
    The ravenous horde is here,
See them! the crows and vultures,
    Sowers of dire alarms;
Oh! bells, from out your steeples
    Fling forth your call to arms!
        Ring out!   Ring on!   Ring madly
          The valiant Flemish peal!

The fell sword of the troopers —
    Brief triumph shall they know —
Upon your soil ancestral
    E'en now your sons lay low!

But to the ruthless victor
  Your freedom dear you sell,
Proud, dauntless, little nation,
  Whom only numbers quell!
      Ring out! Ring on! Ring sadly
      The noble Flemish peal!

But see! in the dark heavens
  The dawn of justice light!
There to the dim horizon
  The brutal horde takes flight.
The radiant day of glory
  Day of revenge is here,
Oh! bells, proclaim your triumph
  With music loud and clear!
      Ring out! Ring on! Ring proudly
      The free-born Flemish peal.

— From the French of Dominique Bonnaud

THE DRUMS

Permission of the *Evening Bulletin,* Philadelphia

Ere we wonder at his absence, let us tell a little
truth
Of the healthy, careless fellow who epito-
mizes Youth.
We will miss him from the gridiron when the
foot ball season comes
For he left his spirit moving to the music of the
drums;
For he knows that all the knowledge
He can make his own at college
Will not compensate him wholly for the absence
of the drums;
For the rat-tat-tat of drums!
You will miss him from the diamond, the links
and tennis court,
Miss the sport.
He's been summoned by the drums!
By the thrilling call of bugles, by the echoing
report
Of a cannon fired by Rumor where grim Death
is doing sums;
Doing sums with grim precision —
Hell's subtraction and division —
With an abacus of drums;
Not the tiny kettle drums;
Not the snare, or tenor drums;

But the drum fire of the cannon that perpetually
                strums
            With insistent shot and shell
            On the tympanum of Hell.
            But there's music in the drums!
            There is magic in the drums!
            There is music, there is magic,
            There is fascination tragic
                In the drums!

For the drums are telling patriots of wrongs
                that must be righted;
The drums are droning dirges of the lives the
                Hun has blighted;
            Of the blood that he has spilled;
            Of the babies he has killed;
Of the retribution awful that a righteous Lord
                has willed.
            " Boy, we need you! "
                Cry the drums.
            " Though we bleed you,"
                Cry the drums.
            " Free the world as we have freed
                you! "
                Cry the drums.
            " Boy, you're wanted! "
                Cry the drums!
            And, undaunted
            Here he comes!

Hail Columbia's sons are marching!   Rich and
poor alike are chums!
They've been welded fast together by the magic
of the drums!
By the drums!
By the rat-tat-tat
Of drums!
By the fiat flat
Of drums!
By the glory that's surrounding
Every deed of dogged pounding!
Of the roll of honor sounding!
Of the drums!

— GRIF ALEXANDER

FOR FRANCE

Permission of the author

She had been stricken, sorely, ere this came;
  And now they wrote that he, her boy, was
      dead —
  Her only one!   Through blinding tears she
      read,
Trying to see what followed his dear name.
  He had died " gloriously," the letter said,
" Guarding the Tricolor from touch of shame
Where raged the battle furious and wild."
  Catching her breath, she stayed despair's ad-
      vance.
She was a mother; but, besides — a child
          Of France!

And after, though remembrance of past years
  Dulled not to her fond vision nor grew dim;
  Though every slightest incident of him
Was treasured in her breast, she shed no tears.
  Her cup was full now, even to the brim,
And for herself she knew nor hopes nor fears.
So, toiling patiently, with noble pride
  And lifted head she met each pitying glance,
She was the mother of a son who died —
          For France!
              — Florence Earle Coates

NEXT YEAR

Permission of *Everybody's Magazine,* New York

Up and down the street I know,
   Now that there is Grief and War
All day long the people go
   As they went before;

But when now the lads go by —
   Careless look and careless glance —
My heart wonders —" Which shall be
   Still next year in France? "

When the girls go fluttering —
   Flushing cheek and tossing head —
My heart says " Next year shall bring
   Which a lover dead? "

Lord, let Peace be kind and fleet —
   Put an end to Grief and War;
Let them walk the little street
   Careless as before!

             — MARGARET WIDDEMER

THEN GIVE US WINGS

If wings will help our men to see
Some Boche's belching battery,
Unloosing from a screen of trees
Its screeching death upon the breeze —
Or help our giant guns to search
With truer aim each hidden perch
Of Teuton guns, and make them meek,
Ere they again may chance to speak —

If wings, O God, will do these things,
Then give us wings.

If great, destroying wings might stay
Munitions in their hurried way,
Or hold a reënforcement back
By dropping ruin on its track,
Or yet set free the pent-up hell
Of depots filled with shot and shell,
Or swiftly give eternal sleep
To ships that prowl the nether deep —

If wings, O God, will do these things,
Then give us wings and still more wings.

If fast, avenging wings might cast
On German cities such a blast
Of desolating death and pain

As fell again and still again
On England's homes — and thus awake
The heart of pity — and so make
An end to killing mothers, wives,
And maiming helpless infant lives —

If wings, O God, will do these things,
Then give us wings, and wings and wings
And still more wings.

If dauntless, daring wings that dash
O'er No-Man's Land, with shot and crash,
Might beat back wings that would assail
Advancing armies with their hail —
If dauntless wings like these that ride
O'er No-Man's Land, might turn the tide
Of great offensive — bring about
Allied success and Teuton rout —

If wings, O God, will do these things,
Then give us wings and wings and wings
Devouring wings that cleave and soar,
And yet more wings and more and more!

If multitudes of wings might rise
To blind aggression's lustful eyes,
And render powerless every stroke
That seeks to force the tyrant's yoke —
If multitudes of wings might give

Democracy a chance to live,
And make this bloody carnage cease,
And bring to earth a lasting peace —

If wings, O God, will do these things,
Then give us wings, and wings and wings,
And still more wings arrayed to smite
Till Vict'ry come — the hosts of light
Beneath the sun, whose pinions shine
Beyond our farthest battle line!

— ANTHONY EUWER

IN FLANDERS FIELDS

Permission of the *New York Times*

In Flanders fields the poppies blow
Between the crosses, row on row,
That mark our place; and in the sky
The larks still bravely singing fly,
Scarce heard amidst the guns below.
We are the dead.   Short days ago
We lived, felt dawn, saw sunset glow,
Loved and were loved, and now we lie
    In Flanders fields.

Take up our quarrel with the foe,
To you from failing hands we throw
The Torch — be yours to hold it high;
If ye break faith with us who die,
We shall not sleep, though poppies grow
    In Flanders fields.
— Lieutenant-Colonel John McCrae

THE SERVICE FLAG

Permission of the author

Dear little flag in the window there,
Hung with a tear and a woman's prayer;
Child of Old Glory, born with a star —
Oh, what a wonderful flag you are!

Blue is your star in its field of white,
Dipped in the red that was born of fight;
Born of the blood that our forebears shed
To raise your mother, The Flag, o'erhead.

And now you've come, in this frenzied day,
To speak from a window — to speak and say:
" I am the voice of a soldier-son
Gone to be gone till the victory's won.

" I am the flag of The Service, sir;
The flag of his mother — I speak for her
Who stands by my window and waits and fears,
But hides from the others her unwept tears.

" I am the flag of the wives who wait
For the safe return of a martial mate,
A mate gone forth where the war god thrives
To save from sacrifice other men's wives.

" I am the flag of the sweethearts true;
The often unthought of — the sisters, too.

I am the flag of a mother's son
And won't come down till the victory's won!"

Dear little flag in the window there,
Hung with a tear and a woman's prayer;
Child of Old Glory, born with a star —
Oh, what a wonderful flag you are!
                          — WILLIAM HERSCHELL

PEACE WITH A SWORD

By permission of the author

Peace! How we love her and the good she
      brings
  On broad, benignant wings!
And we have clung to her, how close and long,
  While she has made us strong!
Now we must guard her lest her power cease,
And in the harried world be no more peace.
     Even with a sword,
     Help us, O Lord!

For us no patient peace, the weary goal
  Of a war-sickened soul;
No peace that battens on misfortune's pain,
  Swollen with selfish gain,
Bending slack knees before a calf of gold,
With nerveless fingers impotent to hold
     The freeman's sword.
     Not this, O Lord!

No peace bought for us by the martyr dead
  Of countries reeking red;
No peace flung to us from a tyrant's hand,
  Sop to a servile land.
Our Peace the State's strong arm holds high
     and free,
" The placid peace she seeks in liberty,"

Yea, " with a sword."
Help us, O Lord!

O Massachusetts!   In your golden prime,
   Not with the bribe of time
You won her; subtle words and careful ways
   In perilous days.
No!   By your valor, by the patriot blood
Of your brave sons poured in a generous flood;
      Peace, with a sword!
      Help us, O Lord!

Bring out the banners that defied a king!
   The tattered colors bring
That made a nation one from sea to sea
   In godly liberty.
Unsheathe the patriot sword in time of need,
O Massachusetts, shouting in the lead,—
      " Peace with a sword!
      Help us, O Lord! "

                              — ABBIE FARWELL BROWN

SQUARING OURSELVES

How many howled about Josephus every time a
    sailor man
Found àn unresponsive barkeep when he went
    to rush the can!
How they growled about Josephus when com-
    manders got the news
That the Admiral had orders for a dry and
    boozeless cruise!
Even such a wild teetotaller as the temperate
    T. R.
Shouted from a thousand housetops that Jo-
    sephus went too far.
From all quarters of the Nation excellent, well-
    meaning folk,
Said in letters to the papers that Josephus was
    a joke.

Poets chuckled (we among them) in all sorts of
    jibing verse
When Josephus said that seamen might be
    brave, and still not curse.
Never on the rolling ocean had men navigated
    ships
Be the weather fine or dirty, without oaths upon
    their lips.
Even Dr. Lyman Abbott had to pause and
    breathe a prayer

For a man who said that sailors had not simply
    got to swear!
And there swept across the Nation, North and
    South and East and West
The unanimous conclusion that Josephus was a
    jest.

But when Congress started peering into things
    that had to do
With the arming of the warship and the com-
    fort of the crew,
When grave statesmen asked him questions as
    to this and as to that
It was noticed that Josephus answered right
    straight off the bat.
For his drinkless, curseless navy — every unit
    — thanks to him,
From the dreadnoughts to the cutters, is in first-
    class fighting trim.
Now at last the pitying jesters (we among
    them) see a light,
For the fact has dawned upon us that Josephus
    is all right!

                  — JAMES MONTAGUE

THE WOUNDED SOLDIER IN
THE CONVENT

What is that clanging noise I hear
    Through the still convent ringing?
It is the carriage-ambulance
    A wounded soldier bringing.

Upon his coat the blood-spots shine;
    He limps — a shell has caught him —
His gun he uses for a crutch,
    Descending, to support him.

A veteran he, with fierce moustache —
    The triple stripes he's wearing —
All prudes and hypocrites he loathes,
    And starts by loudly swearing.

Well-nigh insulting are his looks,
    With ill-bred gibes he rallies
The novices — beneath their caps
    They blush at his coarse sallies.

If at his side, thinking he sleeps,
    The sister breathes a prayer,
Straightway astir he fills his pipe
    And whistles a bored air.

What use to him their faithful watch,
    The care that never ceases?

He knows his leg is lost and done,
    And he'll be hacked to pieces.

He's very angry — Let him be!
    Here no one knows impatience,
There reigns an atmosphere that soothes
    And cows the rudest patients.

Slow is the spell, but sure, that wields
    This band, to service given,
With fingers soft they touch the wounds,
    And softly speak of Heaven.

So subtle is their pious charm,
    Our grumbler soon will see it
In his own way — and to each prayer
    Make the response, " So be it! "
                    — FRANCOIS COPPEE

HARVEST IN FLANDERS

In Flanders' fields the crosses stand —
Strange harvest for a fertile land!
Where once the wheat and barley grew,
With scarlet poppies running through.
This year the poppies bloom to greet
Not oats nor barley nor white wheat,
But only crosses, row by row,
Where stalwart reapers used to go.

In Flanders' fields no women sing,
As once they sang, at harvesting;
No men now come with scythes to mow
The little crosses, row by row.
The poppies wonder why the men
And women do not come again!

In Flanders, at the wind's footfall,
The crosses do not bend at all,
As wheat and barley used to do
Whenever wind went running through.
The poppies wonder when they see
The crosses stand so rigidly!

O God, to whom all men must bring
What they have done for reckoning,
At harvest-time what byre or bin
Have you to put these crosses in?

What word for men who marched to sow
Not wheat, but crosses, row by row?

Alas! Our tears can never bring
The men who came here harvesting
And come no more! We do not know
What way the singing women go,
Their songs all still! But crosses stand
Row after row in Flanders land!

— LOUISE DRISCOLL

HAY FEVER

I do not wish the Kaiser ill,
I wish him nothing that would kill,
No bombs with neatness and dispatch
To wipe him from life's kaffe klatch;
No dagger thrust between his ribs,
That would destroy His Royal Nibs;
I would not have him swiftly die,
That's much too good for such a guy;
I only wish the Kaiser might
Hay Fever get and get it right!

I wish the Kaiser's royal nose
Might know the woes my poor nose knows;
I only wish his royal chest
Might always feel a sore distress,
As mine must feel until the day
October's frost shall come our way.
I wish the royal piece of cheese
Might be forever doomed to sneeze.
Death is too good for such a king,
Hay fever would be just the thing.

A pair of watery eyes and red,
An aching throat and fevered lips;
And then a nose that constant drips,
The wish for sleep, but all in vain;
To end one cough to cough again,

All these are parcel of the wish
I cherish for that royal fish,
If I could work my will sublime,
He'd suffer till the end of time.

I'd never let the Kaiser die,
Although for death he'd often cry,
For punishment for all he's done,
His nose it would forever run,—
A million years on earth he'd stay
And sneeze a million times a day.
Sweet sleep would never find his bed,
All night alone the floor he'd tread,
Death is too good for such a king,
Hay fever would be just the thing!

     — ANONYMOUS

IN SAN FRANCISCO

Permission of the author

Aw, gee, I wisht them ol' fog-horns would stop blowin'. Sounds just like some one moanin'; an' gosh, I feel blue enough to-night without them howlin' around down there.

I ain't never been no Jane for showin' feelin's. I've always had the sand to buck it off. But aw, to-night I'm wopped between the lamps. I got to git this off my chest — it's jist bustin' me. Don't get me wrong. I ain't no weak mouth; but I ain't got no mother, never had no father, ain't got nobody to spill to — But he left to-night — had to beat it to France or somewhere wid de army. Course I knowed he was billed to go sometime, but ain't it funny you don't seem to feel it in your bones that they are sure goin' till — bang! They're gone.

To-night Sam came steppin' up. That's his name — Sam. Gosh, I just love that name. Well, Sam comes up. Gee! you ought to see Sam; he is the grandest lookin' guy you ever lamped — all shoulders an' no waist. Say, all the skirts on de coast wuz crazy for him, an' gosh, he grabs me an' sticks.

Well, Sam he comes up an' says, "Honey kid, I's got some headlines in big print. To-morrow we are off for de big fight. We've bin called into service."

"Aw, Sam — Sam honey, to-morrow?" I says.

Then I felt myself kinda slippin', so I put on the brakes. I ain't no sob artist like them swell dames up the drag. It's a bunch of nerve an' grit I's got. We set down an' chewed the rag about things; then he sed:

"Honey kid, I guess there ain't much chanst of me gittin' back; this ain't no joy ride we're goin' on. We're goin' to lick them Germans, an' we ain't comin' back till we do. I ain't never had no yellow streak, so I'm there to the last ditch.

"Now, listen, darlin'. I want you to promise Sam somethin'. You ain't like the roughnecks around here. Now, kid, don't go sinkin' down wid them. Gosh, when I'm gone they ain't goin' to be nobody to look after you, honey, so you gotta buck in an' do it yerself. 'Tain't gonna be no soft job. This ain't no ladies' seminary round here, an' there's always a lot of rough guys hornin' in. You jist hang onto that grit of yours, an' you'll be there a million. Maybe the ol' luck will fasten on me an' I'll get back all together."

Gosh! I couldn't hang on any longer, so I turned her loose. I jist bawled like a brat.

I tried to laugh an' tell him I'd be all to the hunky when he wuz away, but I didn't git along very well through the waterfall.

Purty soon Sam slid down offa the couch on his knees by me, wid his head in my lap. His big shoulders were jist shakin', an' he said:

" May, darlin', when I'm gone, I wisht at night, before yer go to yer pallet, you would try an' say a little prayer fer me. Will you, baby? You've been all the happiness an' sunshine I've ever had."

An' I says: " Sam, I ain't never heard no swell prayers, an' I don't know the real way they do it; but if God will listen to me say it my own way, without no frills or fancy kneelin', oh gosh, Sam, I'll beg Him to take care of yer, darlin'."

Then I pulled him up, an' I sat on his lap. We tried to kid a little — you know, when your heart is achin', you try to act it ain't at all.

Purty soon I thought of somethin'. On my finger I had a ring — no sets or glass: jist a big ring wid a lot of carvin's on it. It wuz my mother's — I ain't never had it off, hungry or no hungry. But I took it off my mit, an' slipped it on Sam's little finger, an' sed: " Sam darlin', I want you to wear this li'l ring of mine; an' at night, when yer down in them trenches in ' No Man's Land,' an' you're feelin' purty lonesome, just touch this li'l ring, an' you will know I am wid you, kid, lovin' you an' thinkin' about my Sam."

He kissed the li'l ring — gosh! it wuz regular Francis X. an' Mary Pickford stuff; only dis wuz the real thing; we wuz jist about breakin' our hearts in that li'l sketch.

Then Sam looked at the Big Ben an' sed, " Gosh, I gotta be goin', honey."

We walked over to the door. He put his arms around me, not sayin' a word, an' kissed me jest as silent, then quick he turns an' says: " So long, honey," an' wuz gone.

I stood an' watched him; but this ramble-shackle palace ain't set in grounds, so I could only see him goin' down the hall.

I ain't much fer size — never weighed a hundred in my life: jist a li'l rat,— but I've got to stick out my chest an' buck up. But before I git so fresh wid myself I'm goin' to have a good ol' bawl all to myself, an' I'm not goin' to leave none fer to-morrow. I'm gonna go down to de water early in de mornin', an' I might lamp 'em when they're sailin' away. None of de gang has never saw me bawl yet, an' they ain't agoin' to now.

Gosh! I wisht them ol' fog-horns would stop blowin': they'd make any guy shaky.

— BERNADINE HILTY

OUR YOUTH

Permission of the author

Once more, once more into the fire they go,
 With their dreamed and their undreamed
  deeds of the coming years
Put to the chance of a shell or a bayonet's
 blow —
 With a smile in their eyes made bright by a
  touch of tears,
And a laugh on their lips they have gone to
 meet our foe!

Once more the flag that they love floats proudly
 on ahead
 Which never on land or sea has known de-
  feat
And the voices that rise from the unforgotten
 dead
 Sing the great song that lifts at the marching
  feet,
That it ever has flung its folds where Freedom
 led!

To-day they fight for a freedom newly born,
 For the earth is weary of kings and the
  spawn of kings,
And out of the throes of a world with anguish
 torn

Shall rise a peace no glory of conquest
    brings,
Like the peace that came to the earth on
    Christmas morn.

For this they fight and not for an inch of land
    Or the dollars wrung from a foe by the cards
    of state!
Thank God he has placed at our helm a stead-
    fast hand
    And an eye that can look unmoved on the
    face of Fate
And a will that can dare and a heart that can
    understand!

He has sent our best to the world's last great
    crusade,
    They shall not come back till the world at
    last is free!
For the Old World calls to the New, and, un-
    afraid,
    Our youth go forth to their fame and their
    agony,
For God will judge in the end, and His price be
    paid!

                 — ARTHUR HOBSON QUINN

THE UNFURLING OF
THE FLAG

Permission of the author

There's a streak across the sky line
   That is gleaming in the sun,
Watchers from the light-house towers
Signaled it to foreign Powers
   Just as daylight had begun,
      Message thrilling,
      Hopes fulfilling
   To those fighting o'er the seas.
" It's the flag we've named Old Glory
   That's unfurling to the breeze."

Can you see the flashing emblem
   Of our Country's high ideal?
Keep your lifted eyes upon it
And draw joy and courage from it,
   For it stands for what is real,
      Freedom's calling
      To the falling
   From oppression's hard decrees.
It's the flag we've named Old Glory
   You see floating in the breeze.

Glorious flag we raise so proudly,
   Stars and stripes, red, white and blue,
You have been the inspiration
Of an ever-growing nation

Such as this world never knew.
      Peace and Justice,
      Freedom, Progress,
   Are the blessings we can seize
When the flag we call Old Glory
   Is unfurling to the breeze.

When the cry of battling nations
   Reaches us across the space
Of the wild tumultuous ocean,
Hearts are stirred with deep emotion
   For the saving of the race!
      Peace foregoing,
      Aid bestowing,
      Bugles blowing,
   First we drop on bended knees,
Then with shouts our Grand Old Glory
   We set flaunting to the breeze!
                  — CLARA ENDICOTT SEARS

MARCHING FORTH TO WAR

Permission of the *Chicago Examiner,* Chicago

It was grand to be a soldier and go swinging
    down the street
With a crowd of cheering children throwing
    flowers at your feet,
While the girls along the sidewalk waved to
    you a fond good-by,
And the prettiest of them, maybe, had a tear
    drop in her eye.
Bands were playing, flags were waving, when
    the army marched away,
It was glorious and thrilling, but it's pretty grim
    to-day.

Down the streets you file at midnight, not a soul
    to see or hear,
Not a strain of martial music, not a flutter not a
    cheer.
No one there to breathe a blessing on the cause
    you go to fight,
Or to wish you all the glory of a battle for the
    right.
Gloom and silence all around you, gloom and
    silence on before.
Ah! it sure does take a hero thus to march away
    to war.

It was fine to be a soldier, when the ship sailed
    down the bay,
And the shores were filled with people come to
    watch you sail away.
How the whistles shrieked and shouted on the
    boats that passed you by,
How the echoing farewell salvos rose until they
    reached the sky.
How you thought of deeds of valor as you
    watched the vessel's bow
Cut the waves that tumbled seaward. Ah!
    It's grimmer business now.

In the darkness of the morning, just before the
    break of dawn,
On the silent decks you huddle as the vessel
    hurries on.
One by one you see the fading of the lights
    along the shore,
And you hear the swash and rustle of the water,
    nothing more.
Like an exile you must stand there and look out
    across the foam.
Ah! it takes a heart of iron thus to sail away
    from home.

THE SPIRIT OF '17

Used by permission of the *Atlantic Monthly,* Boston

En route from Fort Ethan Allen, Vermont, to Detroit, whither my husband was ordered to join his base hospital, we were delayed in Ithaca, New York. While waiting in the hotel lounge, I chanced to overhear an interesting conversation.

I had noticed a fine-looking man near me, reading the morning paper: he was distinctly the very prosperous city business man, his well-kempt appearance bespoke culture, money, and intelligence. While I was occupied with my speculations about him, a young man, just a boy, in fact, came in. He was a well-set-up chap, with the fresh healthy skin and clear-eyed eagerness of a country lad. He had never been far from the up-country farm where they raised the best breeds of livestock. He couldn't have given a college yell to save his life, and he was innocent of fraternity decorations and secrets. Just the kind of boy I would like to have call me " mother." His clothes were good, but evidently from the general store of the small town. He carried a good-sized box, which he put across his knees as he seated himself. I knew that it was his luncheon which mother had packed, and that it included fried chicken and cold home-made sausage, cakes, sand-wiches, fried cakes, crullers, mince pie and cheese, apples and winter pears; and a few relishes besides. Why, I could smell the luncheon that my mother had put up for my brother forty years ago.

The Boy gazed all around, took in each detail of the room and its furnishings, with all the quiet dignity and interest of a well-born American country youth. You know a real Yankee country boy isn't like any other; there is a balance, an understanding, that is natural. It is inborn to be at home in any surrounding, however new and strange, so long as it is real.

After the Boy had surveyed the room, he looked over at the man reading. He sat perfectly still a few minutes, then " Oh hummed," and waited again, and fidgeted a bit; but no-body spoke. I could see that he was fairly bursting with news of something. Finally, to the man, " Can you tell me how far it is to Syracuse, sir? "

" Well,"— lowering his paper,—" not exactly, but three or four hours, I'd say. Going to Syracuse? "

" Yes, I've enlisted. I passed one examination, but I'm going to Syracuse for another and then I'm going to Spartansburg. Senator Wadsworth says, and it looks that way to me, that it is just as much our fight as theirs, and we ought to have been in it three years ago; they are getting tired over there. I'd hate to be drafted. I'd feel mean to think I had to be dragged in; besides I want to do my part. Every fellow ought to get into it."

" What part of the service did you elect? "

" The infantry, sir. I'm going to Spartansburg to the training-camp." Silence for some moments; then, showing that his bridges were burned, " I've sold my clothes; sold 'em for four dollars and I'm to send 'em right back soon's I get my uniform. I hope I don't have to wait for the soldier clothes. I think I got a good bargain and so did the fellow I sold 'em to. I thought I wouldn't need 'em while I was in the army, and when I got back they'd be all out of style; and then — I may never come back." A ripple of seriousness passed over his boyish face. " But it was a good chance and I took it. Have you a son, sir?"

" Yes, I have a son just eighteen, at Cornell. He expects to go next year if they need him in the aviation."

" I'm just nineteen. I thought I'd better enlist. It's just possible they might draft 'em later, and I just couldn't stand it to be drafted. Do you think I'll be able to go home for Thanksgiving? " he asked eagerly.

" I wouldn't think quite so soon. You'll hardly get there by that time."

" Well, I think I can go home for Christmas, don't you? " And a shade of anxiety crept into his tone. " I live up the road here a way, — Wellsville, you know, about forty miles. Don't you think I'll get to Syracuse to-night if I go right on? I'd like to get through so I could be ready for work to-morrow morning. I don't want to waste any time now that I'm all ready."

The Boy settled back with a look of forced patience, and the man held up his paper again; but I could see that he was not reading, and there was a look of suffused sadness in his face.

The Boy had taken from his pocket a pair of big, dark-blue, home-knitted mittens; on the palms was sewn red woolen to reënforce them. He carefully drew them on, folded his hands, thumbs up, on his luncheon-box, edged to the front of his chair, and sat thinking with eyes fixed on the far-away places of his dream. He was going over it all again; there was no haste, no excitement, no foolish sentiment, but sure determination and the courage of youth suddenly turned to manhood. With a little start he came back to the present, and, rising, said, " I guess I'd better be going. You said I could get a train in about half an hour? "

" Before you go, will you tell me, my boy, why you chose the infantry? "

" Well, when you read of anything real hard that has to be done you will notice that it is always the infantry that does it. They have to be strong, young fellows they can depend on for the real hard things. So I chose the infantry, sir."

There was a silence, which he broke with the quiet words, " I think I'll be going. Good-by, sir."

Springing from his chair, the man grasped the boy's hand. " God bless you, son, and good luck! "

With misty vision we both stood and watched him out of sight; then, with all previous convention of acquaintance forgotten as we looked into each other's eyes, the man said, " It is the spirit of '17 gone to the colors."

— MARY HERRICK SMITH

IN WARTIME

By permission of the author

Long years I longed for them, for the young
  faces,
The golden hearts, that other women fold
Securely in their hands' and hearts' em-
  braces —
I, empty-hearted with no hand to hold.
      But now, but now — surely I am the one
      Who sleeps in peace knowing she hath no
      son.

The summoning flag unfurled has stilled the
  aching
I lived with many years; the drum, the fife,
Bid me be glad that for their pitiless taking
I have no treasure of young golden life.
      And yet, and yet — last night I lay awake,
      I had no peace for other women's sake.

The flying flag shows dimly through their weep-
  ing,
But in their voices sounds the bugle's voice,
While I, with no young gold for gift or keep-
  ing,
Sit by my empty coffers and rejoice. . . .
      Not so, not so — to-night I am the one
      Who cannot sleep for that she gives no
      son.
            — MRS. SCHUYLER VAN RENSSELAER

THE MISCREANT

By permission of the author

It was a slender Belgian lad,
A child to make a father glad,
Negligent, he stood beside
The highway, stretching white and wide;
Thence had come but yesterday
The Uhlans riding on their way;
And now was heard, in steady beat,
A rising sound of marching feet.
They came, a mass of gray pulsating,
Steady-moving, palpitating,
On with unrelenting tread:
Spiked the helmet on each head,
Straight each gun, each eye, each stride,
Each belt, each knapsack coincide,
A bayonet rattled at each side.

The word rang, " Halt," and at the sound
The rifle butts thud on the ground.
" Come here, my boy," the Captain cried,
" Last night, a certain Belgian died;
And why, would'st know? that Belgian lied.
Now, tell me, thou, and tell me true —
Lest such a fate befall thee, too —
Look squarely at me, hold thee still:
Lie Belgian troops on yonder hill? "
The boy nor flinched nor caught his breath,

He knew a glorious lie meant death,
But looked the Captain in the eye
And said, " Nay, none are there, or nigh."
The conclusion of my story
Comes from a letter amatory,
Which one Fritz, in school-boy hand,
Wrote Gretchen in the Fatherland.

" Wouldst believe it, Gretchen, that boy lied;
The little traitor! he defied
Our Kaiser and the German race!
Dear me! that thoughts so black and base
Should harbor in so sweet a face! "

And then Fritz told in close detail,
With many an expletive and wail,
How his company was mauled
By Belgian guns.   What else he scrawled,
I spare the reader, both his fight
And courtship.   He concludes:

                              " That night
We stood that boy against a wall,—
It was a church, as I recall.
He would not let us bind his eyes
Or tie his hands.   We looked for cries,
For tears and pleadings for reprieve;
But not a word said he, save ' Vive
La Belgique! '   Now could mind conceive

Act more un-German!   Could one believe
Such guilt to Kaiser and to God!
'Twas I, dear, led the shooting squad.
We fired — we all are steady-eyed —
And so the little miscreant died."

Thus wrote Fritz, in school-boy hand,
To Gretchen in the Fatherland.
If such be miscreants, what would I,
Or thou do, so to live, so die?

As for Fritz, there is no pother;
That precious piece of " cannon-fodder "
Was shot while looting with red hand:
And Gretchen weeps in the Fatherland.
                        — Dr. Felix E. Schelling

THE LITTLE ONE-STAR FLAG

By permission of the author

Oh, I used to hear the family
  In the house across the way —
A father, and a mother, and a child.
    And, oh, the noise they used to make;
    They'd keep the neighborhood awake —
I sometimes used to think they'd drive me wild!
    I glanced across the way the other day;
    It seemed too quiet over there, by far.
And hanging in the window of the house across
      the way
    Is a little flag which bears a single star!

There's a Service Flag in Broadway,
  And it flaunts two thousand stars.
Oh, it swings there to the glory
  Of the soldiers and the tars.
But no star there in its beauty
Tells of stronger Love and Duty
    Than the little one-star flag across the way.

Oh, I used to see them waiting
  In the house across the way —
The mother, and a little girl, so sweet.
    And, oh, the way they used to shout;
    And, oh, the way they'd hurry out
When they saw Daddy coming up the street.

Now I miss the noise they made there as they
  played;
It seems too quiet over there by far —
Oh, they're watching from the window of the
  house across the way
  By the little flag that bears a single star!

There's a Wonder Flag in Wall Street,
  Flying from a dizzy height,
Like a gorgeous patch of heaven
  That was ripped from starry night.
But no star there in its beauty
Tells of stronger Love and Duty
  Than the little one-star flag across the way!
                              — DAMON RUNYON

RISE UP! RISE UP, CRUSADERS!

By permission of the author

Never in all the scarlet past
Since God first placed the suns,
Not when the Goths drank deep of blood,
And women feared the Huns,
Not when the hordes of Attila
Made toys of flame and shame,
Came call so clear
For them to hear
Who'd fight in Freedom's name.

Rise up! rise up, crusaders, to meet the hosts
        of Hell!
They prate of Art and Science but they give us
        shot and shell;
They call on God, blaspheming, as they plunge
        their hands in gore;
They've butchered millions, millions, and
        they'd butcher millions more.

What hold they dear who dare the race
To meet the might they wield?
The smile upon a baby's face?
The maid who would not yield?
The faith that men and nations keep
When sacred vows are made?
Why, then, should Europe's women weep?
Why preach we our crusade?

Rise up! rise up, ye stalwart, to save a world
　　from woe!
The Hun is growing boastful.　　We must give
　　him blow for blow.
　　Where Goths and Vandals wake again
From sleep that's ages long
There's madness in the souls of men,
And murder in their song.
They are not men as men are known
To human hearts alone,
Their music is a woman's wail,
Or dying hero's groan.
They crave a world's dominion,
And they come, a wanton flood,
To drown the hope that God gives man
In seas of human blood.

Rise up! rise up, crusaders!
Send forth a clarion cry!
The race shall not be slaves to Huns
Though you and I must die.
A world at war?
A billion men who arm and fight and slay?
What are our blaring bugles for?
Is Man insane to-day?

Not we to whom the call has come,
Not we, the unafraid,
Now arming, God be with us, for the last, the
　　great Crusade;

Nor they who fight our fight with us,
Across the surging sea,
Where men are facing madmen
That all peoples may be free.

— EDWARD VAN ZILE

JUST THINKING

Standin' up here on the fire-step,
  Lookin' ahead in the mist,
With a tin hat over your ivory
  And a rifle clutched in your fist;
Waitin' and watchin' and wond'rin'
  If the Hun's comin' over to-night —
Say, aren't the things you think of
  Enough to give you a fright?

Things you ain't even thought of
  For a couple o' months or more;
Things that'll set you laughin'
  Things that 'ull make you sore;
Things that you saw in the movies,
  Things that you saw on the street,
Things that you're not really proud of,
  Things that are — not so sweet.

Debts that are past collectin',
  Stories you hear and forget,
Ball games and birthday parties,
  Hours of drill in the wet;
Headlines, recruitin' posters,
  Sunsets 'way out at sea,
Evenings of pay days — Golly —
  It's a queer thing, this memory!

Faces of pals in homeburg,
  Voices of women folk,
Verses you learnt in school days
  Pop up in the mist and smoke
As you stand there grippin' that rifle,
  A-starin', and chilled to the bone,
Wonderin' and wonderin' and wonderin',
  Just thinkin' there — all alone!

When will the war be over?
  When will the gang break through?
What will the U. S. look like?
  What will there be to do?
Where will the Boches be then?
  Who will have married Nell?
When's that relief a-comin' up?
  Gosh! But this thinkin's hell!

                    — HUDSON HAWLEY

THE STARS

Can it be possible that these same stars,
That smile in heavenly beneficence
Upon the dewy reaches of the fields,
And shadows of the quiet, sleeping woods,
Shine, too, on Europe's throes of agony?
Yea, even so, and God be thanked 'tis so,—
On War's red death the quiet stars look down
And on the trenches clear Orion beams
As fair as o'er the spires of Coventry;
Some lonely lad from Normandy, perchance,
Or son of far America, may catch
With dying eyes the twinkling Pleiades,
And see in them the old sweet walks of home;
Antares' gleam, Capella's golden light
Speak but one tongue, need no interpreter:
But more, to every doubting heart they speak,
While empires rock, and earth and air and sea
Drink heedlessly the priceless blood of youth,—
God still His watch must keep; the stars still
      shine!

— Agnes McConnell Sligh

MY SON

God gave my son in trust to me;
Christ died for him, and he should be
A man for Christ.   He is his own,
And God's and man's; not mine alone,
He was not mine to " give."   He gave
Himself that he might help to save
All that a Christian should revere,
All that enlightened men hold dear.

" To feed the guns! "   O torpid soul!
Awake, and see life as a whole.
When freedom, honor, justice, right,
Were threatened by the despot's might,
With heart aflame and soul alight,
He bravely went for God to fight
Against base savages, whose pride
The laws of God and man defiled;
Who slew the mother and her child,
Who maidens pure and sweet defiled.
He did not go " to feed the guns,"
He went to save from ruthless Huns
His home and country, and to be
A guardian of democracy.

" What if he does not come? " you say;
Ah, well!   My sky would be more gray,
But through the clouds the sun would shine,

And vital memories be mine.
God's test of manhood is, I know,
Not " Will he come? " but " Did he go? "
My son well knew that he might die,
And yet he went, with purpose high,
To fight for peace, and overthrow
The plans of Christ's relentless foe.

He dreaded not the battle-field;
He went to make fierce vandals yield.
If he comes not again to me
I shall be sad; but not that he
Went like a man — a hero true —
His part unselfishly to do.
My heart will feel exultant pride
That for humanity he died.

" Forgotten grave! "　This selfish plea
Awakes no deep response in me,
For, though his grave I may not see,
My boy will ne'er forgotten be.
My real son can never die;
'Tis but his body that may lie
In foreign land, and I shall keep
Remembrance fond, forever, deep
Within my heart of my true son
Because of triumphs that he won.
It matters not where any one
May lie and sleep when work is done.

It matters not where some may live;
If my dear son his life must give,
Hosannas I will sing for him,
E'en though my eyes with tears be dim.
And when the war is over, when
His gallant comrades come again,
I'll cheer them as they're marching by,
Rejoicing that they did not die.
And when his vacant place I see
My heart will bound with joy that he
Was mine so long — my fair young son —
And cheer for him whose work is done.

— DR. JAMES D. HUGHES

SALUTATORY

Our honor 'tis who stay behind —
   Soldiers of France's glory —
To hail with strengthening words and kind
The men that march the foe to find,
   And rout him from our hallowed soil
   That groans with pain of his despoil —
      His menace gory.

Our honor 'tis to hold you dear,
   War-men of skill and soul;
The old, the young, alike revere —
Men faring forth who smile at fear,
   While earth itself returns with dread
   The echo of their martial tread
      Toward triumph's goal.

Our honor 'tis to nurse you well —
   Soldiers of newer glory —
To bind your wounds and soothe your brow,
   Who little dreamed to add as now
   By faith and nerve the valorous meed
   Of high, unselfish, mighty deed
      To France's story .

Our honor 'tis to give our tears —
   Soldiers that lie at rest!

Smiles we give, too, and cheering glance
With farewell kiss, while saddened France
  To men asleep in reddened fields
  The peace unending gently yields
    Of Heaven's blest.
            — ANGELE MARAVAL-BERTHOIN

ONLY A VOLUNTEER

Permission of the author and the *Independent,* Kansas City

Why didn't I wait to be drafted
And led to the train with a band,
And put in a claim for exemption,
Oh, why didn't I hold up my hand?
Why didn't I wait for a banquet,
Why didn't I wait for a cheer;
Why didn't I wait to be drafted
Instead of a volunteer?

And nobody gave me a banquet,
Nobody said a kind word;
The puff of the engine,
The grind of the wheels,
Was the only good-by I heard,
Then off to the camp I hustled
To be trained for the next half year,
And in the shuffle forgotten;
I was only a volunteer.

Perhaps some day in the future,
When my little boy sits on my knee
And asks what I did in the Great War,
And his little eyes look up at me,
I will have to look back into those eyes
That at me so trustingly peer
And tell him I wasn't drafted,
I was only a volunteer.

— CORPORAL RICHARD D. IRWIN

THE SAILOR-MAN

Permission of *Life,* New York

I like the look of khaki and the cut of army
    wear,
And the men of mettle sporting it, at home and
    over there;
But there's something at the heart-strings that
    tautens when I meet
A blue-clad sailor-man adrift, on shore-leave
    from the fleet.

From flapping togs his sea-legs win some tinge
    of old romance
That's proper to the keeper of the paths that
    lead to France;
For what were all the soldiers worth that ever
    tossed a gun
Without the ships and sailor-men to pit them
    'gainst the Hun!

There's sunlight now and steady ground be-
    neath the sailor's tread,
And every pleasure beckons him, and every
    snare is spread;
Speed well this visitor, whose home 'twixt heav-
    ing decks is set,
Whose playmates are the darkness, and the
    bitter cold, and wet!

His comrades these; his foe is ours, the foe of
    law and right,
The stealthy, murderous German " fish," that
    prowls and kills by night;
And none may sink him where he swims, flout-
    ing God's age-built plan,
None but the guardian of us all, the rolling
    sailor-man.
His hands are often cruel cold; his heart is
    oftener warm,
For in its depths he knows 'tis he that shields
    the world from harm;
Because I know it too, my heart beats warmer
    when I meet
A blue-clad sailor-man adrift, on shore-leave
    from the fleet.

— M. A. DeWolfe Howe

THE COST

Permission of *Everybody's Magazine,* New York

Six o'clock when the homeward traffic of a
city is heaviest from shops and offices. The
street was crowded with people who, in their
rush, bumped heedlessly against each other.
Some smiled. Some went with fixed faces like
masks. Motor-horns and car-bells blared and
clanged in a medley of impatient sound.
Through it all I wove my way — a little shuttle
trailing my one frail.thread through the pattern
of the whole.

Then I heard him bawling of the wares he
sold.

"Here you are!" he cried, his mouth in-
credibly big and twisted. "Here you are!
Buy the American colors! Red! White!
Blue! The colors that never run! Be a
patriot! Buy your little Service-pin! Here
you are!"

I stopped before him.

"How much are the Service-pins?" I asked.

"How many stars do you want on it?" said
he, plunging his hand into the bag of them
strung round his neck with a strap.

"Three," I told him proudly.

He held out the pin to me — a white square
rimmed with red, three blue stars on its field;

each star for one man of my blood who risks his life for America.

"It costs fifteen cents," said he; "a nickel a star."

Through a sort of haze I stared at him. "Fifteen cents!" he had said. "A nickel a star."

And suddenly I seemed to see the oldest of the three: a desk-bound man with straight and pleasant lips and the comfortable ways of one who is happy among simple things. There had been no yearning for adventure, no restlessness. Yet how quickly he had gone just the same. Like a child, who hears a loved one calling him, he had closed his books and risen to answer — at once. One long look into steady eyes very like his own. Only one question: "You want me to go, Mother?" And the cry in answer: "My boy!"

And the other one — the second; he who is so gentle that babies nod wisely at him, as though there were some secret between them. I remember the winter's night he brought the stray kitten home and fed it with warm milk, drop by drop. Already his comrades in the Signal Corps complain because his horse follows him inside their tent. A man so generous that his touch holds a kind of healing. Yet he too has gone — to kill! Gone with the warmth of his heart blazing white hot from his eyes. When last I saw him, it seemed to me he was an arrow strung back on the bow to the head. The change in him!

Then the last to go — the youngest, the tallest, the straightest; his brows a little knit — puzzled — not wholly understanding this thing that told him to put his boyhood behind him and become, too soon, a man. Still, eager, frightened, and very brave — he went.

These stars of mine " A nickel a piece; The three of them for fifteen cents! " I thought I laughed. But maybe not, for through the dusk the vender peered at me strangely. Then —

" Can't pay? " he asked. " Too much? "

I fastened my Service-pin to my breast.

" No," I said. " I can pay. It costs a lot, but — not too much."

— ETHEL LLOYD PATTERSON

THE EYES OF WAR

Permission of the author

Like a gauzy speck in the pearling dawn,
  We drift through the silent skies,
Over No-Man's-Land, where the smoke balls
    spawn
  And the deadly gases rise.
We mark the spot where the battery stands —
  Where sappers toil in the trench-scarred
    height.
We map each mile of a hostile land,
  Where millions writhe in battle-blight.

No silvery bugle to speed our flight,
  Nor the flutter of banners gay;
Not a war steed's stamping for the fight,
  As we rise at break of day.
Only the song of the wind in the planes —
  A thrill that lives in the day-dawn's glow —
A shifting vision of country lanes,
  That wave like ribbons below.

—CHART PITT

FILE THREE

File Three stood motionless and pale,
   Of nameless pedigree;
One of a hundred on detail —
   But would I had been he!

In years a youth, but worn and old,
   With face of ivory;
Upon his sleeve two strands of gold —
   Oh, would I had been he!

The General passed down the line,
   And walked right rapidly,
But saw those threads and knew the sign —
   Oh, where was I, File Three!

" Twice wounded? Tell me where you
     were."
   The man of stars asked he.
" Givenchy and Lavenze, sir "—
   Oh, where was I, File Three!

Then crisply quoth the General:
   " You are a man, File Three."
And Tommy's heart held carnival —
   God!   Would I had been he!

THE SOLDIER

Permission of the author

He needs no tinsel on his coat,
    No medal, star or braid;
No outward sign of rank or worth
    To keep him unafraid.

The soldier carries in his breast
    A living accolade —
The dear medallion of her face,
    The noblest medal made!

Her faith, her hope, her tenderness,
    Her human fear and pain
Are like the glory on his soul
    To comfort and sustain.

In honor and in pride he goes
    To face his duty grim;
Transplanted to himself, he feels
    The heart that beats for him!
                    — CHRISTOPHER MORLEY

OUR GIFT

Permission of the author

Behold Thy sons, O Lord!
We give them back to Thee,
With outstretched arms and bleeding hearts,
On bended knee.
Wrought in Thy image, nurtured in Thy truth,
The brave, the strong, all-glorious in youth;
Guard this our priceless gift, in strife and
    stress,
O Lord of Righteousness!

Our noblest sons, O Lord!
We give them back to Thee.
Use them to glorify Thy name,
A ransom for the free.
Yet as we give Thee back Thine own to-day,
On bended knee with fervent hearts we pray,
Guard Thou our valiant sons on land and sea,
O Lord of Liberty!

            — CAROLINE TICKNOR

ASLEEP BY THE IRISH SEA

Permission of the author

To France!   How many weary miles,
Dear lads, it seemed! but only smiles
We flung to speed your brave Crusade,
Why stain with tears your accolade?
     But, ah, we feared the swirling foam!
     The wail of winds that sob and moan!

In dreams, that stirred the lonely night,
We saw the flash of steel's white light,
We heard the cry of men at bay,
In anguish watched the dreadful fray.
     We saw, in dreams, the fields run red,
     We groped in fear 'mid tumbled dead.

Gone now our hopes and dreams and fears,
We live with grief that stabs and sears,
Yours not the trench — the blinding flame,
Not yours the scarlet road to fame.
     Yours but to stand, with quickened breath,
     At grave salute — to challenge Death.

Yours but to close Life's doors, swung wide,
And cross, with song, the Great Divide!
Sweetly you rest, by Larne's gray sea,
The booming surf your threnody.
     Sleep on, brave lads!   A world set free,
     Shall thy immortal guerdon be!
                    — ELIZABETH GLENDENNING RING

COLUMBIA COMES

Permission of the author

In war's fast deepening shades Columbia stood
And watched Democracy's descending star.
She heard with pity Belgium's dying cry,
Whose rape by Germany made Satan blush.
When her own children died by German blasts
While in their merchant ships on lawful seas,
Columbia felt the rub of future chains,
And saw Death write with steel his awful name
Across the flags of all her cherished kin.
Then Liberty's bright torch lit well her path,
At whose far-distant end is destiny;
She saw her Lincoln keeping anxious watch.
And now, the troops of seventeen seventy-six,
In battle cry, are charging in her soul.

Presumptuous Germany! to make a foe
Of her whose birth was of throne-shaking war
That threw the Western walls of Empire down;
Who first hitched lightning to her spacious car
And in it pioneered the undersea;
Who saddled first the untamed steeds of air
And rode them at her will through lofty
      heavens;
Whose tireless mind still cleaves new seas of
      thought;
Whose fearless feet still march to Freedom's
      drums.   — THOMAS MEEK BUTLER

A NATION'S PRAYER FOR STRENGTH
TO SERVE

Make bare thy mighty arm, O God, and lead this people on.

Day by day, month after month, we have prayed that the cup of war might pass from us, for we have not been able to say thy will, not ours, be done.

We have gazed with awe upon the horrors of the battlefields of Europe. There we have seen suffering and death such as the angels of heaven never looked down upon before; while here we have enjoyed the peace and prosperity which have flooded our land, and we have prayed that we might not have to give up our comfort and our ease and face the awful realities of war. We have said to our souls, thou hast much goods laid up, eat, drink and be merry and think not of duty, but of pleasure.

We have not prayed, O God, that thou wouldst show us our duty and give us strength to follow wherever thou mightst lead, but we have prayed that our will might be thy will. We have prayed that thou wouldst save us from suffering, not that thou wouldst give us strength to meet and bear suffering if called by thee to do our part in saving civilization from destruction.

Forgive us, O Lord God Almighty, that we have so long prayed not to know the path of duty, but to be kept in the path of ease and safety.

We cannot fathom the mysteries of this world, we cannot understand how evil can for so long a time master good; we cannot see how out of all the horrors and sufferings of these latter years thou canst bring forth blessings to mankind and get glory and honor unto thyself. But we know, O Divine Father, that all things shall work together for good to them that love and serve thee. Teach us then to love thee as we have never loved thee before, teach us to serve thee as we have never served thee in the past.

We believe that thou art calling us to take up our cross and follow thee, and that thou hast called us to some great service to mankind and to thyself.

Arm us, O God, with the power of right.

Let us not go forth trusting in our own strength, which is but weakness. Let no spirit of revenge, no hatred fill our hearts, but give us the strength which comes from seeking to know and to do thy will, and from being led by thee.

Grant, O Father, that we may be ready to drink of the cup from which thy Blessed Son, our Redeemer, drank, when, in boundless love for others, he prayed that not his will, but thine, be done. Draining the cup of human agony, he became the Savior of mankind, redeeming the world from the power of evil through his suffering, death and resurrection. He taught us that service and sacrifice are better than great riches, that he who seeks selfishly his own good only may lose his own soul.

What shall it profit us as a nation to gain the wealth of the world and to lose the soul of our honor and of our duty to thee?

If such be thy will, may it be ours as a nation to be led by thee to help save mankind from the dominion of evil.

Give unto us, O God of infinite love, thy " grace, which is love outloving love," to enable us to say where thou leadest we will follow.

Make us a nation, O thou Almighty Ruler of Nations, worthy to become the redeeming power to save mankind from sinking beneath the barbarism which fights against civilization, against human liberty and against thee, that all the nations of the earth shall come to know thee and to seek thy guidance through all the ages to come unto thy honor and glory.

OLD GLORY

Permission of the author

A group of stars on an azure field —
There the bond of the Union stands revealed;
With bars of red and bars of white,
That spurn the earth and seek the light —
'Tis the flag that men have died for!

That star-flecked banner marked the line
From Bunker Hill to Brandywine;
We fancy that its bars of red
Proclaim the blood our grandsires shed,
For this is the flag they died for!

It graced the heights of Monterey;
It fluttered at Manila Bay.
"The flag is there!"   Thus ran the news
From Pekin and from Vera Cruz —
And this is the flag they died for!

Blow on o'er land; blow on o'er sea,
O starlit banner of the free;
Though foes abound and tyrants rave,
Blow on, O banner of the brave!
And this is the flag we'll die for.

— George B. Hynson

SCREENS

They put a screen around his bed;
    A crumpled heap I saw him lie,
White counterpane and rough dark head,
    Those screens — they showed that he would
        die.

They put the screens around his bed;
    We might not play the gramophone,
And so we played at cards instead
    And left him dying there alone.

The covers on the screen were red,
    The counterpanes were white and clean;
He might have lived and loved and wed,
    But now he's done for at nineteen.

An ounce or more of Turkish lead,
    He got his wounds at Suvla Bay;
They've brought the Union Jack to spread
    Upon him when he goes away.

He'll want those three red screens no more,
    Another man will get his bed;
We'll make the row we did before
    But — Jove! — I'm sorry that he's dead.
                      — W. M. LETTS

EFFICIENCY

By permission of the author

I

For forty years he plotted,
  For forty years he planned,
His ships on every ocean,
  His spies in every land;
He perverted social progress,
  He exploited poor men's thrift,
He " utilized " the princeling
  And the human wreck adrift.
There was naught for him too trifling,
  Or too great for him to wrench,
He corrupted press and pulpit,
  Even Justice on the bench;
The maid who dressed my lady
  The man who drove her car,
The statesman in the senate,
  And the men who lead in war.

And yet for all his well laid trains,
  For all the fires he fanned,
For all the things he bought and sold,
  And all the plots he planned:
He shall not pull it off, my boy,
  He can not put it through,
He's up against a world in arms
  Of fearless men and true.

II

Forty years of preparation,
   All at a tyrant's will,
For forty years, a nation
   In one eternal drill;
His furnaces ablazing
   With case of mighty guns,
Shipyards crammed with seacraft
   And dreadnaughts, tons on tons;
Learn'd men concocting poison,
   Devising gun and snare,
To ruin a friendly neighbor
   And slay him unaware.
No enemy was moving,
   No flag of war unfurled,
He plotted 'gainst a peaceful,
   An unsuspecting world.

And yet for all his well-laid trains,
   For all the fires he fanned,
For all the things he bought and sold.
   And all the plots he planned:
He shall not pull it off, my boy,
   He can not put it through,
He's up against a world in arms
   Of fearless men and true.

III

For three years now you've beaten him,
  In sky, on earth, at sea,
Briton, Frenchman, Belgian,
  And the men of Italy;
He boasted he'd sack Paris,
  The Marne proved that boast vain,
He names no more Verdun nor Somme,
  He's beaten on the Aisne.
And now 'tis for America
  To join the valiant line,
To run him from his cover,
  Back to the river Rhine.
If you had plotted forty years
  To murder your nearest friend,
What would you think if your success
  Attained no better end?

Foiled, disgraced, bankrupt, and bled,
  Despised: now God forefend,
If this be not for " efficiency "
  A very sorry end.
He shall not pull it off, my boy,
  He can not put it through,
He's up against a world in arms
  Of fearless men and true.
                    — DR. FELIX E. SCHELLING

SEVEN DAYS' LEAVE

Bravely acted, little lady;
Bravely acted, wife of mine.
Though I know your heart is aching
Almost to the point of breaking,
Not a word of what you're feeling,
Only just a teardrop stealing.
Such a splendid little lady,
Such a splendid wife of mine!

Bravely spoken, little lady;
Bravely spoken, wife of mine.
Just a tightening of your fingers
While your hand in mine still lingers;
Just " God bless and keep you, dearest;
In my thoughts you're always nearest."
Such a sportsman, little lady;
Such a sportsman, wife of mine!

Is it fair, my little lady?
Fair to you, O wife of mine?
Seven days we two together,
Then we part, perhaps forever.
(God! those days, though only seven,
Seemed a little glimpse of Heaven!)
That's the question, little lady.
Yours the answer, wife of mine.

— CAPTAIN BLACKALL

THE STAR SPANGLED BANNER —
WITH VARIATIONS

I

Oh, say, can you sing from the start to the end
What so proudly you stand for when orchestras
    play it —
When the whole congregation, in voices that
    blend,
Strike up the grand hymn, and then torture and
    slay it?
How they bellow and shout,
When they're just starting out! —
But " the dawn's early light " finds them
    flound'ring about
'Tis The Star Spangled Banner they're trying to
    sing,—
But they don't know the words of the precious
    old thing.

II

Hark, " the twilight's last gleaming " has some
    of them stopped,
But the valiant survivors press onward serenely
To " the ramparts we watched," where some
    others are dropped,
And the loss of the leaders is manifest keenly.
Then " the rocket's red glare "

Gives the bravest a scare,
And there's few left to face the " bombs bursting in air "—
'Tis a thin line of heroes that manage to save
The last of the verse and " the home of the brave! "

ON TO VICTORY!

Our business is to exert the largest possible fraction of our strength at the earliest possible moment, and then to exert our constantly growing strength so fast as with the utmost energy and efficiency we can develop it, until we win the peace of overwhelming victory. This war, so far as we are concerned, was brought on by German militarism and American pacifism working together. To let either or both of them dictate the peace that is to end it would be an immeasurable disaster. We should not have any negotiations with those who committed and who glory in the Lusitania infamy, the rape of Belgium, and the hideous devastation and wholesale murders and slavery in the conquered countries. We are fighting for the fundamental sanctities of life and decencies of civilization. We are fighting for the liberty of every well behaved nation, great or small, to have whatever government it desires and to live unharming others and unharmed by others. We are sending our troops to fight abroad so that they may not have to fight at home. Germany must be beaten, and the Prussianized militaristic autocracy of the Hohenzollerns humbled or the world will not be safe for liberty-loving peoples. We must fight this war through to victory no matter what the cost in time or money or in the blood of our bravest and dearest.

The ultimate task of our young men of to-day is so to lead the generation now coming on the stage that this nation shall assure its international safety by grasping and acting on the fundamentals of duty. I sincerely believe that on the whole we of this nation have a little finer material on which to work than is true of any other nation; that in our land there are better ideals than elsewhere of the duty of men and women to one another, to their neighbors, to their country, and to the world at large. I do not see how any man can go through the camps where our army is now being trained without feeling a thrill of pride in the manliness, energy and resourcefulness of the men who are there slowly acquiring not only the bodies of soldiers but the feelings of patriots. Those camps are to-day the great universities of American citizenship, and we ought to make them permanent features of our national life. There could be no finer material for citizenship than that afforded by the men and women of this nation.

We can be sure that our armies at the front and that our fleets and squadrons will do well and **bravely**, and that we shall hold our heads

high because of their valor. Theirs is the great task, theirs will be the great glory. Let us who stay behind back them in every way!
— THEODORE ROOSEVELT

MIZPAH

Permission of *Munsey's Magazine,* New York

Oh, man o' mine in olive drab,
So handsome, brave, and strong,
You're bound for " somewhere " there in
    France
To join the fighting throng.

Oh, man o' mine, from out your heart
Your eye speaks brave and true;
You'll do your patriotic part,
For, man o' mine, that's you!

For liberty you're going, man,
And honor — therefore go!
But oh, my man, come back, come back,
Because I need you so!

One man in ten must fall they say;
Each hour my fervent prayer
Will seek its heavenward way to plead
That God may guard you there.

I know the horrors you will see;
I hear the bursting shell.
But, man o' mine, you'll do your part,
And do it more than well!

'Tis such as you they want, my man,
To stem the tyrants' greed;
But oh, my man, come back, come back,
My love, my strength, my need!

— GERTRUDE STEWART

THE FLAG

Permission of the author

O some sing Tipperary,
　Some sing the Marseillaise,
And some prefer God Save the King,
　Or other martial lays;
Give me the Spangled Banner,
　With its stars now fifty fold,
I love our Spangled Banner,
　For we sang that song of old.

Some love the brave tricolor,
　And some the Union Jack,
Some hail the flag of Italy,
　Or the yellow, red and black;
They're all our friends and allies,
　Stout men, alert and bold,
But I love the Spangled Banner,
　'Tis the flag we waved of old.

Flag of our faith and freedom,
　Flag for which we've bled!
Flag of our home and happiness,
Flag of our honored dead!
No tyrant's sword shall wound thee,
　No alien hand shall hold
Our loved Star Spangled Banner,
　The flag we loved of old.
　　　　　　— Dr. Felix E. Schelling

"HONEY" DRAWS THE LINE

I've beamed when you hollered " Oh, Girlie! "
I've hopped when you bellowed " Oh, say! "
I've fallen for " Dearie," and " Missus,"
   And everything else till to-day.
But there's one thing that's got to be different,
From now till the Great War is done —
Unless you're prepared for a riot,
   You've got to quit calling me " Hun! "

MARY

Permission of the *Yale Review,* New Haven, Conn.

Mary! I'm quite alone in all the world,
Into this bright sharp pain of anguish hurled.
Death's plunged me deep in hell, and given me
    wings
For terrible strange vastnesses; no hand
In all this empty spirit-driven space; I stand
Alone and whimpering in my soul.   I plod
Among wild stars, and hide my face from God.
God frightens me. He's strange. I know
    Him not,
And all my usual prayers I have forgot:
But you — you had a son — I remember now.
You are not Mary of the virgin brow.
You agonized for Jesus.   You went down
Into the ugly depths for him.   Your crown
Is my crown.   I have seen you in the street,
Begging your way for broken bread and meat:
I've seen you in trams, in shops, among old
    faces,
Young eyes, brave lips, broad backs, in all the
    places
Where women work, and weep, in pain, in
    pride.
Your hands were gnarled that held him when
    he died,

Not the fair hands that painters give you,
   white
And slim.   You never had such hands: and
   night
And day you labored, night and day, from child
To woman.   You were never soft and mild,
But strong-limbed, patient, brown-skinned from
   the sun,
Deep-bosomed, brave-eyed, holy, holy One!
I know you now!   I seek you, Mary!   Spread
Your compassionate skirts; I bring to you my
   dead.

This was my man.   I bore him.   I did not
   know
Then how he crowned me, but I felt it so.
He was my all the world.   I loved him best
When he was helpless, clamoring at my breast.
Mothers are made like that.   You'll under-
   stand
Who held your Jesus helpless in your hand,
And loved his impotence.   But as he grew
I watched him, always jealously; I knew
Each line of his young body, every tone
Of speech; his pains, his triumphs were my own.
I saw the down come on his cheeks, with dread,
And soon I had to reach to hold his head
And stroke his mop of hair.   I watched his
   eyes

When women crossed his ways, and I was wise
For him who had no wisdom.   He was young,
And loathed my care, and lashed me with
  youth's tongue.
Splendidly merciless, casual of age, his scorn
Was sweet to me of whom his strength was
  born.
Besides, when he was more than six feet tall
He kept the smile he had when he was small.
And still no woman had him.   I was glad
Of that — and then — O God!   The world
  ran mad!
Almost before I knew this noise was war
Death and not women took the son I bore!

You'll know him when you see him: first of all
Because he'll smile that way when he was small.
And then his eyes!   They never changed from
  blue
To duller gray, as other children's do,
But, like his little dreams, he kept his eyes
Vivid, and very clear, and vision-wise.
Seek for him, Mary!   Bright among the ghosts
Of other women's sons he'll star those hosts
Of shining boys.   (He always topped his class
At school.)   Lean forward, Mary, as they
  pass,
And touch him.   When you see his eyes you'll
  weep

And think him your own Jesus.   Let him sleep
In your deep bosom, Mary, then you'll see
His lashes, how they curl, so childishly;
You'll weep again, and rock him on your heart
As I did once, that night we had to part.
He'll come to you all bloody and bemired,
But let him sleep, my dear, for he'll be tired,
And very shy.   If he'd come home to me
I wouldn't ask the neighbors in to tea. . . .
He always hated crowds. . . . I'd let him
    be. . . .

And then perhaps you'll take him by the hand,
And comfort him from fear when he must stand
Before God's dreadful throne; then, will you
    call
That boy whose bullet made my darling fall,
And take him in your other hand and say —
" O God, whose Son the hands of men did slay,
These are Thy children who do take away the
    sins of the world. . . ."
— IRENE McLEOD

PRESIDENT WILSON'S FLAG DAY
ADDRESS

Washington, D. C., June 14th, 1917

My Fellow Citizens:

We meet to celebrate Flag Day because this flag which we honor and under which we serve is the emblem of our unity, our power, our thought and purpose as a nation. It has no other character than that which we give it from generation to generation. The choices are ours. It floats in majestic silence above the hosts that execute those choices, whether in peace or in war. And yet, though silent, it speaks to us — speaks to us of the past, of the men and women who went before us and of the records they wrote upon it. We celebrate the day of its birth; and from its birth until now it has witnessed a great history, has floated on high the symbol of great events, of a great plan of life worked out by a great people. We are about to carry it into battle, to lift it where it will draw the fire of our enemies. We are about to bid thousands, hundreds of thousands, it may be millions, of our men, the young, the strong, the capable men of the nation, to go forth and die beneath it on fields of blood far away — for what? For some unaccustomed thing? For something for which it has never sought the fire before? American armies were never before sent across the seas. Why are they sent now? For some new purpose, for which this great flag has never been carried before, or for some old, familiar, heroic purpose for which it has seen men, its own men, die on every battlefield upon which Americans have borne arms since the Revolution?

These are questions which must be answered. We are Americans. We in our turn serve America, and can serve her with no private purpose. We must use her flag as she has always used it. We are accountable at the bar of history and must plead in utter frankness what purpose it is we seek to serve.

It is plain enough how we were forced into the war. The extraordinary insults and aggressions of the Imperial German Government left us no self-respecting choice but to take up arms in defense of our rights as a free people and of our honor as a sovereign government. The military masters of Germany denied us the right to be neutral. They filled our unsuspecting communities with vicious spies and conspirators and sought to corrupt the opinion of our people in their own behalf. When they found that they could not do that, their agents diligently spread sedition amongst us and sought to draw our own citizens from their allegiance — but some of those agents were men connected with the official Embassy of the German Government itself here in our own capital. They sought by violence to destroy our industries and arrest our commerce. They tried to incite Mexico to take up arms against us and to draw Japan into a hostile alliance with her — and that, not by indirection, but by direct suggestion from the Foreign Office in Berlin. They impudently denied us the use of the high seas and repeatedly executed their threat that they would send to their death any of our people who ventured to approach the coasts of Europe. And many of our own people were corrupted. Men began to look upon their own neighbors with suspicion and to wonder in their hot resentment and surprise whether there was any community in which hostile intrigue did not lurk. What great nation in such circumstances would not have taken up arms? Much as we had desired peace, it was denied us, and not of our own choice. This flag under which we serve would have been dishonored had we withheld our hand.

For us there is but one choice. We have made it. Woe be to the man or group of men that seeks to stand in our way in this day of high resolution when every principle we hold dearest is to be vindicated and made secure for the salvation of the nations. We are ready to plead at the bar of history, and our flag shall wear a new luster. Once more we shall make good with our lives and fortunes the great faith to which we were born, and a new glory shall shine in the face of our people.

THE BELGIAN FLAG

Red for the blood of soldiers,
   Black, yellow and red —
Black for the tears of mothers,
   Black, yellow and red —
And yellow for the light and flame
Of the fields where the blood is shed!

To the glorious flag, my children,
   Hark! the call your country gives,
To the flag in serried order!
He who dies for Belgium lives!

Red for the purple of heroes,
   Black, yellow and red —
Black for the veils of widows
   Black, yellow and red —
And yellow for the shining crown
Of the victors who have bled!

To the flag, the flag, my children,
   Hearken to your country's cry!
Never has it shone so splendid,
   Never has it flown so high!

Red for the flames in fury,
   Black, yellow and red —

Black for the mourning ashes,
Black, yellow and red —
And yellow of gold, as we proudly hail
The spirits of the dead!

To the flag, my sons! Your country
With her blessing " Forward " cries!
Has it shrunken? No, when smallest,
Larger, statelier, it flies!
Is it tattered? No, 'tis stoutest
When destruction it defies!

— From the French of E. CAMMAERTS

FLY A CLEAN FLAG

By permission of the author and the publishers, The Reilly &
Britton Co., Chicago

This I heard the Old Flag say
As I passed it yesterday:
" Months ago your friendly hands
Fastened me on slender strands
And with patriotic love
Placed me here to wave above
You and yours.   I heard you say
On that long departed day:
' Flag of all that's true and fine,
Wave above this house of mine;
Be the first at break of day
And the last at night to say
To the world this word of cheer:
Loyalty abideth here.'

" Here on every wind that's blown,
O'er your portal I have flown;
Rain and snow have battered me,
Storms at night have tattered me;
Dust of street and chimney stack
Day by day have stained me black,
And I've watched you passing there,
Wondering how much you care.
Have you noticed that your flag,
Is to-day a wind-blown rag?

Has your love so careless grown
By the long neglect you've shown
That you never raise your eye
To the symbol that you fly?"

" Flag, on which no stain has been,
'Tis my sin that you're unclean,"
Then I answered in my shame.
" On my head must lie the blame.
Now with patriotic hands
I release you from your strands,
And a spotless flag shall fly
Here to greet each passer-by.
Nevermore shall Flag of mine
Be a sad and sorry sign
Telling all who look above
I neglect the thing I love.
But my flag of faith shall be
Fit for every eye to see."

— EDGAR A. GUEST

THE OLD ROAD TO PARADISE

Permission of the author and the publisher,
Good Housekeeping, New York

Ours is a dark Eastertide, and a scarlet spring,
But high up at Heaven's gate all the saints sing,
Glad for the great companies returning to their
    King!

Oh, in youth the dawn's a rose, dusk an
    amethyst,
All the roads from dusk to dawn gay they wind
    and twist,
The old road to Paradise, easy it is missed!

But out on the wet battlefields few the roadways
    wind,
One to grief, one to death — no road that's
    kind —
The old road to Paradise, plain it is to find.

(St. Martin in his Colonel's cloak, St. Joan in
    her mail,
King David with his crown and sword — oh,
    none there be that fail —
Along the road to Paradise they stand to greet
    and hail!)

Where the dark's a terror-thing, morn a hope
    doubt-tossed,

Where the lads lie thinking long, out in rain
and frost,
There they find their God again, long ago they
lost.

Where the night comes cruelly, where the hurt
men moan,
Where the crushed forgotten ones whisper
prayers alone,
Christ along the battlefields comes to lead His
own.

Souls that would have withered soon in the
world's hot glare,
Blown and gone like shriveled things, dusty on
the air,
Rank on rank they follow Him, young and
strong and fair!

Ours is a sad Eastertide, and a woeful day,
Yet high up at Heaven's gate the saints are all
gay,
For the old road to Paradise —'tis a crowded
way!

— MARGARET WIDDEMER

AS THEY LEAVE US

Permission of the author

Bid farewell with pride,
  Show no trace of sorrow;
Smile into their eyes,
  Though your courage borrow;
There will be another day,
  And a time
    To pay!

Gallant is their look,
  But their hearts are tender.
Cry aloud your faith!
  Loyal tribute render!
For they go — the young, the brave —
  Liberty
    To save!

Tell them not of fear;
  Whisper not of sadness;
Overbrim to-day
  With heroic gladness;
Let your love, remembered, shine
  As a light
    Benign!

Simple is their trust,
  But 'tis deep as ocean;

Lofty is their hope,
  Selfless their devotion;
And they go — the young, the **brave** —
  Liberty
    To save!

Hark!   The bugles call!
  Wave your banners! — cheer **them**!
Happy, let them dream
  All that's valiant near them!
They will know, when far from **you**,
  That the dream
    Was true!

— Florence Earle Coates

"WE ARE OF ONE BLOOD"

Two nations, but one people, in our color, race
    and creeds,
Who boast a common heritage and sires of
    noble deeds;
They say a line divides us, but, despite the land
    or flood,
We clasp the hand from land to land, for we're
    of common blood.

We may differ as to tariff rates, waters and
    boundary line,
If we catch each other poaching, we will in-
    dicate the fine,
But we think that we should emphasize, 'twill
    do us all much good,
Our fathers came from common soil; their veins
    flow common blood.

When warring nations question us, we'll fling
    the message back,
With stars and stripes entwined about our dear
    old Union Jack,
" We're brothers born, we're brothers still, and
    brothers aye shall be,
We'll stand for right, we'll stand for truth and
    Christian liberty."

The call for world-wide freedom has put us to
  the test,
The price we pay is very high, we're giving of
  our best;
From college, farm and factory, we've sent our
  bravest sons,
To hold our treasured liberty from devastating
  Huns.

To guard our women's honor and our dear old
  native sod,
From war-mad Prussian officers, whose passion
  knows no God.
Our sons have never faltered; they've always
  won the day,
In face of overwhelming odds, they've held the
  foe at bay.

Here's to the sons of Uncle Sam, who stand
  with Jack Canuck,
Who struggle for a righteous cause in good or
  evil luck,
Whose bugles never sound retreat, who fight to
  win or die,
That Stars and Stripes with Union Jack for
  freedom's cause may fly.

And when the war is over and democracy is
  saved,

While we review the gallant crew, who land
    and water braved,
On the North Sea or Langemarck, Vimy or
    Passchendaele,
We'll tell the world, with flag unfurled, " they
    weathered every gale."

And when the noble veteran troops come
    marching through our street,
And loud hurrahs are sounding to the tramping
    of their feet,
The tear drops glistening in some eyes voice
    words we cannot speak,
That God, who holds " our boys " in trust, His
    promise will keep.

            — REV. C. L. McIRVINE

THE TRUMPET CALL

Permission of the author

I dreamed last night of the trumpet-call:
" Come over and help us across the sea,
Come over and help us, brothers all,
We fight for justice and liberty ! "
But my couch was soft and my comforts dear,
And the ones I loved had naught to fear,
So I sent this answer across the sea:
" The sons of France shall fight for me,
Russia's arms and the British fleet
Will shelter me in my safe retreat,
Italy's brave are in the field,
And Canada's troops will never yield."

Again in the darkness I heard a call:
" Come over and help us in the fight,
For the cause of freedom we give our all,
In the name of honor and truth and right ! "
But my heart was sick with desperate strife,
And I clung to peace as this nation's life.
So I sent my answer across the sea:
" The sons of France shall die for me,
Russia's arms and the British fleet,
Will guard this nation against defeat,
Italy's troops are staunch and strong,
And Belgium's faith shall conquer wrong."

Out of the East came a piercing cry:
" 'Tis you in your safe retreat who die!
Alive are the sons of France to-day,
O'er the British fleet death ho' us no sway,
Russia's arms, and Italy's brave,
The valor of Belgium strong to save,
These the immortal standards bear,
You are the dead men over there
In the land made free by the blood of France,
Boasting the Briton's inheritance,
Strong with the strength of every land,
Your fair flag droops in a nerveless hand."

At dawn I rose with my soul aflame,
And I flashed this message across the deep:
" With the living nations enroll my name!
Brothers, we waken from our sleep;
From stately mansion and workshop small,
From mine and mill and college hall,
From mountain and valley and river town,
Men of this nation are winding down.
Sons of France, we will fight to-day!
Fight for the debt we long to pay,
Fight for the valiant British fleet
Guarding our nation from defeat."

And when at last on some glorious morn,
The Peace of a ransomed world is born,
And immortal standards in triumph wave,

Over the heads of the free and the brave,
Glory of France and Britain's pride,
With the Stars and Stripes shall be side by side.

— CAROLINE TICKNOR

THE MAN WHO CAN FIGHT
AND SMILE

Permission of the author

There is need in the world of men to-day
  For the man who can fight and smile;
For the man who can to the field away
  With a song on his lips the while.

There is need in the world of women to-day
  For the woman who smiles and gives;
Who can hide her tears and her deep dismay,
  While in sorrow she works and lives.

There are tears enough in the world to-day,
  With its strife and bloodshed and grief;
We must lift our hearts from the clouds of
    gray,
  And so glimpse the sunshine brief.

We must fight with a faith as well as a will,
  For faith will make victory sure;
With the knowledge that right shall triumph
    still,
  And bring a peace to endure.

So here's to the man who can fight and smile,
  And the woman who smiles as she gives;
And here's to the end of war's dreadful night
  And the dawn of the peace that lives.

— NORMA BRIGHT CARSON

MAKERS OF THE FLAG

This morning, as I passed into the Land Office, The Flag dropped me a most cordial salutation, and from its rippling folds I heard it say: "Good morning, Mr. Flag Maker."

"I beg your pardon, Old Glory," I said, "aren't you mistaken? I am not the President of the United States, nor a member of Congress, nor even a general in the army. I am only a Government clerk."

"I greet you again, Mr. Flag Maker," replied the gay voice, "I know you well. You are the man who worked in the swelter of yesterday straightening out the tangle of that farmer's homestead in Idaho, or perhaps you found the mistake in that Indian contract in Oklahoma, or helped to clear that patent for the hopeful inventor in New York, or pushed the opening of that new ditch in Colorado, or made that mine in Illinois more safe, or brought relief to the old soldier in Wyoming. No matter; whichever one of these beneficent individuals you may happen to be, I give you greeting, Mr. Flag Maker."

I was about to pass on, when The Flag stopped me with these words:

"Yesterday the President spoke a word that

made happier the future of ten million peons in Mexico; but that act looms no larger on the flag than the struggle which the boy in Georgia is making to win the Corn Club prize this summer.

" Yesterday the Congress spoke a word which will open the door of Alaska; but a mother in Michigan worked from sunrise until far into the night, to give her boy an education. She, too, is making the flag.

" Yesterday we made a new law to prevent financial panics, and yesterday, maybe, a school teacher in Ohio taught his first letters to a boy who will one day write a song that will give cheer to the millions of our race. We are all making the flag."

" But," I said impatiently, " these people were only working ! "

Then came a great shout from The Flag:

" The work that we do is the making of the flag.

" I am not the flag; not at all. I am but its shadow.

" I am whatever you make me, nothing more.

" I am your belief in yourself, your dream of what a People may become.

" I live a changing life, a life of moods and passions, of heart breaks and tired muscles.

" Sometimes I am strong with pride, when

men do an honest work, fitting the rails together truly.

"Sometimes I droop, for then purpose has gone from me, and cynically I play the coward.

"Sometimes I am loud, garish, and full of that ego that blasts judgment.

"But always, I am all that you hope to be, and have the courage to try for.

"I am song and fear, struggle and panic, and ennobling hope.

"I am the day's work of the weakest man, and the largest dream of the most daring.

"I am the Constitution and the courts, statutes and the statute makers, soldier and dreadnaught, drayman and street sweep, cook, counselor, and clerk.

"I am the battle of yesterday and the mistake of to-morrow.

"I am the mystery of the men who do without knowing why.

"I am the clutch of an idea, and the reasoned purpose of resolution.

"I am no more than what you believe me to be and I am all that you believe I can be.

"I am what you make me, nothing more.

"I swing before your eyes as a bright gleam of color, a symbol of yourself, the pictured suggestion of that big thing which makes this nation. My stars and my stripes are your dream and your labors. They are bright with cheer, brilliant with courage, firm with faith, because you have made them so out of your hearts. For you are the makers of the flag and it is well that you glory in the making."

— FRANKLIN K. LANⸯ

FATHER AND SON

Permission of the author

I

THE FATHER

Would God that I could go in place
Of him, my hope of house and race.
Would I could shoulder knapsack, gun
Against the wild and furious Hun.
Would I could face the tempest, rain,
The bullets, hunger, thirst and pain.
I'd revel in the maddest fray,
If only he, my boy, could stay.

I would be glad to sink in sea,
Be crucified, or hanged on tree,
Or fall in airplane from the sky.
I've lived.   What matter when I die?
I'd stand, with smiles, in vilest trench,
And laugh at gases, mud and stench.
I would not wail for eyes gone blind,
Or shrink from shatt'ring of the mind,
I'd revel in the maddest fray,
If only he, my boy, could stay.

'Tis ill to know his youthful breast
May be by pallid fear oppressed;

That he may fall in brutal hands
And be a slave to their commands;
That he may shudder, starve and thirst
Among the demon Huns accursed.
Oh, joy, if I could only go
And take the pain and bear the blow!
I'd revel in the maddest fray,
If only he, my boy, could stay.

His boyish flesh is all too fair
To meet the brutes and devils there.
His face it is too glad and bright
To front the demons of the night.
His heart it is too kind and warm
To bear the ice and snow and storm.
Would I for him herewith could go
And bear the pain and face the foe,
I'd revel in the maddest fray,
If only he, my boy, could stay.

II

THE SON

The call to duty now has come;
The flags are out, with fife and drum.
The cause for which we fight is just;
In God above is all our trust.
I gladly go to do my share;

My chance is equal and is fair.
I hope, indeed, that I may live;
In need I have a life to give.

My father long has done his part;
He gave me home and all his heart.
I'd be unworthy of my race
If peril now I dared not face.
My country has done all for me;
I gladly serve to keep it free.
I hope, indeed, that I may live;
In need I have a life to give.

I feel my heart is strong within;
I prize the chance to fight and win.
And if I perish, I but ask
That word come back I did my task.
I'll act so that no blush of shame
Will come to them that bear my name.
I'm happy that, where'er I roam,
My father is secure at home.
I hope, indeed, that I may live;
In need I have a life to give.

—CALVIN DILL WILSON

THE PARADE

Permission of the author

I watch the regiments swinging by
  In the shimmer of polished steel,
With guns that glisten, and flags that fly,
And bronzed young faces, and heads held high,
And the glint of the bayonet finds reply
In the answering flash of the soldier's eye,
  As the endless lines unreel.

I hear the throb of the big bass drum;
  'Tis the heart of the army beats
In its loud tattoo, and my pulses thrum,
And the swelling veins in my temple hum,
And my sight grows dim, and my lips are dumb,
As I stand on tiptoe to see it come
  Through the crowded and cheering streets.

I see the regiments tramping by
  To the lilt of a martial air,
Clean young fellows, alert and spry,
Ready and eager to do and die
For humanity under an alien sky,
And a proud old woman this day am I,
  For my son is marching there!
                              — MINNA IRVING

THE NIGHTINGALES OF FLANDERS

The nightingales of Flanders,
They have not gone to war;
A soldier heard them singing
Where they had sung before.

The earth was torn and quaking,
The sky about to fall;
The nightingales of Flanders,
They minded not at all.

At intervals he heard them,
Between the guns, he said,
Making a thrilling music
Above the listening dead.

Of woodland and of orchard
And roadside tree bereft,
The nightingales of Flanders
Were singing, " France is left! "
— GRACE HAZARD CONKLING

TO FRANCE!

To France! To France! The magic music
        falls
Across the world the voice of God now calls
To France!
The war bells ring, and all the wide world
        gongs,
As soldiers march out with their battle songs
To France!

The bugles and the music of the earth
Call out with joy and marvelous mirth
To France!
To France for God, to France for Liberty
To France for Peace and our Democracy,
To France!

Columbia's hand now lifts the torch of war
And starts with blinding light across the star
To France!
The millions, brilliant, march on down the sky
And great America rings with all the cry
To France!

Come one, come all, to spend your lives and
        gold.
Come heroes, gentlemen, the brave, the bold,
To France!

Come, citizens in khaki, every one,
Come, find your God, come march into the sun,
To France!

To France, to France, the bugles, silver curled,
Go ringing out their chimes across the world
To France!
Come one, come all, the magic music falls,
The voice of God goes ringing with its calls,
To FRANCE!

— EDWIN CURRAN

LANGEMARCK AT YPRES

This is the ballad of Langemarck,
    A story of glory and might;
Of the vast Hun horde, and Canada's part
    In the great, grim fight.

It was April fair on the Flanders Fields,
    But the dreadest April then,
That ever the years, in their fateful flight,
    Had brought to this world of men.

North and east, a monster wall,
    The mighty Hun ranks lay,
With fort on fort, and iron-ringed trench,
    Menacing, grim and gray.

And south and west, like a serpent of fire,
    Serried the British lines,
And in between, the dying and dead,
And the stench of blood, and the trampled mud,
    On the fair, sweet Belgian vines.

And far to the eastward, harnessed and taut,
    Like a scimitar, shining and keen,
Gleaming out of that ominous gloom,
    Old France's hosts were seen.

When out of the grim Hun lines one night,
    There rolled a sinister smoke; —

A strange, weird cloud, like a pale, green
    shroud,
  And death lurked in its cloak.
On a fiend-like wind it curled along
  Over the brave French ranks,
Like a monster tree its vapors spread,
  In hideous, burning banks
Of poisonous fumes that scorched the night
  With their sulphurous demon danks.

And men went mad with horror, and fled
  From that terrible strangling death,
That seem to sear both body and soul
  With its baleful, flaming breath.

Till even the little dark men of the south,
  Who feared neither God nor man,
Those fierce, wild fighters of Afric's steppes,
  Broke their battalions and ran; —

Ran as they never had run before,
  Gasping, and fainting for breath;
For they knew 'twas no human foe that slew;
  And that hideous smoke meant death.

Then red in the reek of that evil cloud,
  The Hun swept over the plain;
And the murderer's dirk did its monster work,
  'Mid the scythe-like shrapnel rain.

Till it seemed that at last the brute Hun hordes
  Had broken that wall of steel;
And that soon, through this breach in the free-
    man's dyke,
  His trampling hosts would wheel; —

And sweep to the south in ravaging might,
  And Europe's peoples again
Be trodden under the tyrant's heel,
  Like herds, in the Prussian pen.

But in that line on the British right,
  There massed a corps amain,
Of men who hailed from a far west land
  Of mountain and forest and plain;

Men new to war and its dreadest deeds,
  But noble and staunch and true;
Men of the open, East and West,
  Brew of old Britain's brew.

These were the men out there that night,
  When Hell loomed close ahead;
Who saw that pitiful, hideous rout,
  And breathed those gases dread;
While some went under and some went mad;
  But never a man there fled.

For the word was " Canada," theirs to fight,
  And keep on fighting still; —

Britain said, fight, and fight they would,
  Though the Devil himself in sulphurous
    mood,
  Came over that hideous hill.

Yea, stubborn, they stood, that hero band,
  Where no soul hoped to live;
For five, 'gainst eighty, thousand men,
  Were hopeless odds to give.

Yea, fought they on! 'Twas Friday eve,
  When that demon gas drove down;
'Twas Saturday eve that saw them still
  Grimly holding their own;

Sunday, Monday, saw them yet,
  A steadily lessening band,
With " no surrender " in their hearts,
  But the dream of far-off land,

Where mother and sister and love would weep
  For the hushed heart lying still; —
But never a thought but to do their part,
  And work the Empire's will.

Ringed round, hemmed in, and back to back,
  They fought there under the dark,
And won for Empire, God and Right,
  At grim, red Langemarck.

Wonderful battles have shaken this world,
   Since the Dawn-God overthrew Dis;
Wonderful struggles of right against wrong,
Sung in the rhymes of the world's great song,
   But never a greater than this.

Bannockburn, Inkerman, Balaclava,
   Marathon's god-like stand
But never a more heroic deed,
And never a greater warrior breed,
   In any warman's land.

This is the ballad of Langemarck,
   A story of glory and might;
Of the vast Hun horde, and Canada's part
   In the great, grim fight.
          — WILFRED CAMPBELL

WHAT IS PATRIOTISM?

Not dilating with pleasurable emotions when the American flag is unfurled. Not rising to our feet when the Star-Spangled Banner is sung. Not joining societies of Colonial Dames, or Daughters of the Revolution. Not sending off fire-works on the Fourth of July. These things may be the expression of civic pride, or of personal pride, or of pure hilarity. They may represent steadfastness of purpose, or mere force of habit. They symbolize contentment in times of peace, and it remains to be seen how far they symbolize nationality in times of peril. For many years no serious obligation has been thrust upon us, no sacrifice demanded of us, in return for protection and security. Now the call is imperative, and by the sustained fervor of our response will the depth and purity of our patriotism be made manifest to the world.

Two things are certain: We were not lightly tossed into this war to appease resentment, or to gratify ambition; and it will take all our energy, sagacity and determination to win out against an adversary whose strength can never be overestimated. Because we are a peace-loving people, we reëlected a profoundly peace-loving President. Because we are a patient people, we endured repeated insult and repeated injury, and sought to win redress by noble but futile remonstrance. Our flag was hauled down on the high seas, our ships were sunk, our seamen drowned like rats. There were many whose hearts were sore over these things, and whose slow-growing anger burned like a hidden flame. There were many who had begun to ask in Lowell's homely words,

> " Wut'll make ye act like freemen?
> Wut'll git your dander riz? "

Still the President's restraining hand held an angry people in leash. Still he hoped against hope, and strove against fate, to obtain some measure of justice. It was only when it became a question of the United States taking orders from Germany, and so yielding our assent to her crimes, that Mr. Wilson asked Congress to proclaim a state of war. We had then no choice left us. It was not merely the nation's honor and the nation's welfare that were at stake. It was the salvation of the nation's soul.

Because we realized this, we read unmoved the appeals sent out by Peace Committees, and Fellowships of Reconciliation. What was the use of asking us to " generate, and set in operation the irresistible energies of love; " to " combat wrong by a sustained appeal to conscience; " to assert " the constructive principles of good-will "? God knows, we had tried to do these things. We had tried, as decent-living men and women, to establish relations of decency with the Central Powers, and we had failed. They struck at us treacherously again and again, plotting in secret at our doors, repaying our hospitality and our trust by making bombs for our destruction on the ships which were sheltered in our ports. It was time, and more than time, that we turned the " irresistible energies of love," the " constructive principles of good-will," to the aid of those allied nations who were bearing on their galled shoulders the burden of a war they had not provoked, and upon whose triumph or defeat rests the hopes of an assaulted civilization.

It is imbecile to prate about the glamor of war and the infection of the military spirit. There is no glamor left in war. We know the truth about it. There is no military spirit, unless it is expressed in Mr. Wilson's words, " The world must be made safe for democracy." No man likes to endure hardships. Few men care to face danger and brave death. This is why we apply the word " heroic " to a nation's defenders. A French soldier, blinded for life in his first skirmish, said quietly in response to commiseration, " Some one had to be there." No simpler exposition of duty was ever given. Some one has to do the hard and bitter work. Some one has to front the peril and bear the burden. The man who says, " Why not I as well as another? " is a patriot. The man who says, " Why not another rather than I? " is a shirker. War is the supreme test of character. It took a war to give us Washington. It took a grievous war to give us Lincoln. Both these men suffered greatly in fulfillment of their high purpose. Both bore their share of pain without shrinking and without resentment.

If we value our civilization, if we love our homes, if we believe that our country stands a living vindication of popular government, we must prove our patriotism in this day of trial. The pacifist talks of peace, the socialist of the tyranny of capital, the sentimentalist of universal brotherhood, the coward of caution. The patriot has a strong and simple word, duty, to guide him on his way. The issue now before us is one which, in the words of Lincoln, " can be tried only by war, and settled by victory." It was not our choice to fight, but the alternative was submission to wrong-doing, and that way lies perdition. American women, no less than American men, repudiated the shameful surrender of all we held sacred and dear, and are now prepared to abide by the consequences of their decision. " Only thus," says Mr. Roosevelt gallantly, " shall we stand erect before the world, high of heart, the masters of our own souls."

— AGNES REPPLIER

THE WRIST WATCH MAN

By permission of the author and the publishers, The Reilly &
Britton Co., Chicago

He is marching dusty highways and he's riding
    bitter trails,
His eyes are clear and shining and his muscles
    hard as nails.
He is wearing Yankee khaki and a healthy coat
    of tan,
And the chap that we are backing is the Wrist
    Watch Man.

He's no parlor dude, a-prancing, he's no puny
    pacifist,
And it's not for affectation, there's a watch
    upon his wrist.
He's a fine two-fisted scrapper, he is pure
    American,
And the backbone of the nation is the Wrist
    Watch Man.

He is marching with a rifle, he is digging in a
    trench,
He is swapping English phrases with a poilu
    for his French;
You will find him in the navy doing anything he
    can,
For at every post of duty is the Wrist Watch
    Man.

Oh, the time was that we chuckled at the soft
    and flabby chap
Who wore a little wrist watch that was
    fastened with a strap.
But the chuckles all have vanished, and with
    glory now we scan
The courage and the splendor of the Wrist
    Watch Man.

He is not the man we laughed at, not the one
    who won our jeers,
He's the man that we are proud of, he's the
    man that owns our cheers;
He's the finest of the finest, he's the bravest of
    the clan,
And I pray for God's protection for our Wrist
    Watch Man.

                — EDGAR A. GUEST

GOD SPEED OUR SOLDIERS

Permission of the author

They know not where the journey ends,
    Our Boys that march away;
They only know their Country sends
    Them on its work to-day.
To foreign lands 'neath alien skies
    The foeman's might to brave —
There Liberty deep-wounded lies
    And calls on us to save.

Ye lads that leave our homes forlorn
    As forth to War ye go,
What though our hearts with grief are torn,
    Yet would we have it so.
Could France — friend of our infancy —
    Appeal to us in vain?
France, that for our liberty bled
    On Yorktown's storied plain!

God speed you, gallant gentlemen,
    Columbia's Chivalry!
Fare forth to fields of Fame again,
    For Faith and Memory.
We know your hearts beat strong and true.
    That Freedom's blood will tell;
Dear Lads, our hats are off to you,
    God keep you all.   Farewell.
                   — GEORGE FREDERIC VIETT

FORGET IT, SOLDIER!

Sometimes when I grow weary
  Of beans and soup and stew,
I long to be where I could get
  A home-cooked meal or two.
Such thoughts as turkey, steaks and chops
  Go floating through my head;
Biscuits, muffins, hot cakes
  And loaves of home-made bread.

    Forget it, soldier!
  Such feasts are not for you.
    Let hunger spice your soup and beans
  And appetize your stew.

At night when I get tired
  Of bed sack, straw and cot;
Of sleeping under blankets,
  Sometimes warm and sometimes not,
I dream of great fourposter beds,
  With pillow, quilt and sheet
And mattresses in which you sink
  About a thousand feet.

    Forget it, soldier!
  Such ease is not for you.
    Let hard work make your bed sack soft,
  As other fellows do.

But worst of all, when I get bored
    With what the fellows say,
I think about a girl I know
    So many miles away;
The nicest, dearest little girl
    You'd ever care to know.
She was my sweetheart once, it seems,
    A hundred years ago.

    Forget it, soldier!
Sweethearts are not for you.
    Your rifle is your sweetheart,
So learn to shoot it true.
                    —C. F. R.— Camp Hancock

LA BASSÉE ROAD

(Guinchy, 1915)

You'll see from the La Bassée Road, on any
　　summer's day,
The children herding nanny-goats, the women
　　making hay.
You'll see the soldiers, khaki clad, in column
　　and platoon,
Come swinging up La Bassée Road from billets
　　in Bethune.
There's hay to save and corn to cut, but harder
　　work by far
Awaits the soldier boys who reap the harvest
　　fields of war.
You'll see them swinging up the road where
　　women work at hay,
The straight long road,— La Bassée Road,—
　　on any summer day.

The night-breeze sweeps La Bassée Road, the
　　night-dews wet the hay,
The boys are coming back again, a straggling
　　crowd are they.
The column's lines are broken, there are gaps
　　in the platoon,
They'll not need many billets, now, for soldiers
　　in Bethune,

For many boys, good lusty boys, who marched
away so fine,
Have now got little homes of clay beside the
firing line.
Good luck to them, God speed to them, the boys
who march away,
A-swinging up La Bassée Road each sunny
summer day.

— PATRICK MACGILL

THE NEW BANNER

O fellow-citizens of storm-tossed lands,
  War weary! Sounds the bugle-note!
    Arise!
New steadfast standards wait your eager
    hands,
  The Star of Promise orbs to meet your eyes.
Great kings must pass, that mankind may be
    free,
Beneath the banner of democracy!

The Mighty Ruler of this mortal life
  Has wisdom, not by mortals understood;
The seeds of blood, the deeds of wanton strife
  Shall some day harvest unexpected good.
Great kings shall pass and every nation be
Ruled by the people — for the people, free.

When the mad anguish of this stricken
    world —
  Where valiant heroes daily fight and fall —
Has passed and Freedom's banners are un-
    furled,
  Then shall we know the reason for it all!
Then every waiting, heart-sick land shall see
The ultimate design of Destiny!

Brave men and women laboring in toil —
  Who, faithful, fight with willing sword or
      pen,
Who work to break the rock or till the soil —
Shall wear the high insignia of men.
All kings must pass, that every man may be
A monarch in his manhood, strong and free!

Beyond the present, unimagined woe,
  A glorious day is breaking o'er the earth:
As spring flowers blossom, after ice-bound
    snow,
  The God of Gods shall bring new things to
    birth.
It is the dawn! Great forces are set free!
All hail the day! World-wide democracy!
                — Katrina Trask

THE COMB BAND

Permission of the author

Oh we love the gay canned music in the watches
    of the night
And we sit about and listen to its records with
    delight,
And we like to hear the music of the regimental
    band
While the leader juggles gayly with the baton
    in his hand,
But the melody that's sweetest as we linger in
    the gloam
Is the harmony extracted from a fine-tooth
    comb.

Yes, we get some tissue-paper and some combs
    from out our kit
And we gather in the squad tent where the
    lantern shadows flit,
And we play a bunch of rag-time with a lot of
    vim and go
In a sort of jazz-band rhythm — all the latest
    stuff we know;
Tunes that set your shoulders swaying, while
    your thoughts are light as foam,
To the sound of syncopation on a fine-tooth
    comb.

It's a crazy sort of music which would drive a
  critic mad
But it makes the evenings shorter, and it really
  ain't so bad,
And it often kind of " gets you " when the boys
  start in to play
For I've seen some homesick fellows wipe a
  tear or two away
To the strains of " Suwanee River " and " My
  Old Kentucky Home,"
As they float in wistful minors from a fine-tooth
  comb.

When this cruel war is over — and I hope I'll
  last it through
And we beat the German army — as we all in-
  tend to do,
When the slaughtering is finished and the final
  fight we win,
And with flags and pennons flying we go march-
  ing through Berlin,
I would like to tramp in triumph past the
  kaiser's palace dome,
Playing " Stars and Stripes Forever! " on a
  fine-tooth comb!

— BERTON BRALEY

TO THE GLORY OF THE NEEDLE

By permission of *Needlecraft,* Augusta, Maine

Never before have they plied so well —
　　Never so sturdily;
　Love in the wool, and there's love in the
　　　stitch,
　And the heart of the woman is doubly rich
Who's knitting for you and me.
The way of the war is a right hard way,
　　And troubled and grim and blind;
But what of the mothers at home to-day,
　　And the love that we left behind?
Click! click! click! — so do the needles sing,
Click! click! click! — souls of us seem a-wing.
　And the gray wool falls into magic place,
　And we fancy we see such a fair, sweet face
　That battle is blessed with a holy grace —
　　And so do the needles sing!

Never before was their task so dear —
　　Never so bitter-sweet!
　We of the trench and the blood-red land
　Look to the thrift of that swift, sure hand
In victory — or defeat!
Our thoughts stray back to a sunlit room
　　Where the casement is wide and bright;
And the fairy work of a finger-loom
　　That spins from the dawn till night.

Click! click! click! — so do the needles croon,
Click! click! click! — with a sort of wistful
        tune;
    And the snow sweeps down from a leaden
        sky,
    And the chill wind whines as it passes by,
    It's a desolate place for a man to die —
        Ah, the needles are none too soon!

Never before was their weave so swift —
        Never so firm and true;
    Love in the parcel that's handed to me,
    Bridging the width of a storm-tossed sea,
And stamped with the seal of YOU!
The gray wool fashions a precious thing,
        That covers a fast-timed heart;
And precious the song that the needles sing
        As they hasten to do their part.
Click! click! click! — so comes the clear re-
        frain,
Click! click! click! — over and over again;
    And it's mother, and sister and maiden fair,
Who knit for the fellow who's " over there,"
        The home-hands, doing their little share
            For the living — and for the slain!

FIRST U. S. SOLDIER DEAD BURIED
IN FRANCE

America's first soldier dead in the war have been buried. Their coffins were draped in the folds of the flag for which they died.

Comrades bore them to the center of a hollow square, formed by American soldiers and veteran French troops. From the massed ranks there stepped a French general. He walked straight to the three coffins, reverently hesitating at the first. Then he stiffened to the salute, doffed his cap, bowed, his face lined as though the mute remains before him were of his own children.

" Private Enright," he said softly, as he bowed before the nearest bier, " Private Gresham "— and he turned to the second — " and Private Hay "— as he turned still further to face the third coffin —

" In the name of France, I bid you farewell. Of your own free will, you left your happy, prosperous country, and took your place by our side.

" You fell facing the foe, in hard, in desperate hand-to-hand fight."

The general hesitated a moment, looked at each of the three flag-draped coffins, and then turned.

" All honor to them," he continued. " Their families should be proud to learn of their deaths.

" We of France ask that the mortal remains of these young men be left with us forever.

" We will inscribe on their tombs:

" ' Here Lie the First United States Soldiers to Fall on French Soil for Liberty and Justice.'

" Passersby will uncover their heads to their graves; men of heart visiting the battlefield will go out of their way to bring their tribute of respect and gratitude.

" Private Enright, Private Gresham, Private Hay — in the name of France I thank you. May God receive your souls.   Farewell! "

A great volley of seventy-fives crashed the final volley of farewell through the leaden, rain-soaked air. Then stalwart American soldiers, tears trickling down their faces, lowered their comrades' remains and covered them over with the soil for which they fought and died.

THE HUN WITH THE GUN

Permission of the author

TO THE KAISER

This is the Thing you have made him —
 A Brute taught to handle a gun;
Bred like a draft ox for muscle,
 Sir'd by Attila, the Hun.

Trained by the gad to obedience,
 To gee and to haw — stop and go;
Robbed of the God-right to reason,
 On driven, blow upon blow.

Taught the vile trick'ry of warfare,
 To glory in rapine and might,
That Christ was all wrong in His Teachings,
 That Treitschke and Neitzsche are right.

King, fear you not that this Terror,
 Blood-maddened, may turn in his pain
And rend you? For is it not written,
 " Who lives by the sword shall be slain "?
                    — WILL P. SNYDER

OUT OF FLANDERS

Three of us sat on the firing-bench
Watching the clouds sail by —
Watching the gray dawn blowing up
Like smoke across the sky.
And I thought as I listened to London Joe
Tell of his leave in town,
That's good vers libre with a Cockney twang;
I'll remember and write it down.

W'en I went 'ome on furlough,
My missus says to me, " Joe,
'Ow many 'Uns 'ave you killed? "
An' I says to 'er, " 'Uns? "
Not thinkin' just wot she meant.
" Yes. 'Uns," she says, " them sneakin', low-
     lived 'Uns! "
Bitter? Not 'arf, she ain't!
An' they're all the same w'y in Lunnon.

My old mate Bill, who's lame
An' couldn't enlist on that account,
'E staked me to a pint of ale
At the Red Lion.   Proper stuff it was
Arter this flat French beer.
" Well, 'ere's to old times! " says Bill,
Raisin' 'is glass,
" An' bad luck to the 'Uns you've sent below! "

'E arsked if I'd shot an' seen 'em fall,
Wanted the de-tails and wanted 'em all!

An' there was my old hoss in Balham,
Gave me a quid w'ich I took, willin' enough,
Altho I made a stall at refusin'.
" That's all right, Joe, boy! Glad to do it!
It ain't much, but it'll 'elp you to 'ave a pleasant
    week,
But w'en you goes back to the trenches,
I wants you to take a crack at the 'Uns fer me!
Get me a German fer every penny in that sov-
    ereign! " 'e says,
Smashin' 'is fist on the table
An' upsettin' a bottle o' ink.
" Lay 'em out! " 'e says;
" Now tell me, 'ow many you killed, about? "

Speakin' o' 'ymns o' 'ate,
They sings 'em in Lunnon, I'm tellin' you
    straight!
You ought to see their faces w'en they arsks
    you about the 'Uns!
Lor' lummy! They ain't arf a bloodthirsty
    lot!
An' the wimmen as bad as the men.
I was glad to get back to the trenches again
W'ere there's more of a 'uman feelin'.

Now, us blokes out 'ere,
We knows old Fritzie ain't so bad as 'e's
    painted
(An' likely, they knows the same about us).
Wot I mean is, 'e ain't no worse than wot we
    are,
Take 'im man fer man.
There's good an' bad on both sides.
But do you think you can s'y anything good
About a German, w'en yer in Lunnon?
Strike me pink!   They won't believe you!
'E's a 'Un, wotever that is,
Some kind o' wild beast, I reckon —
A cross between a snake
An' one o' them boars with 'orns on their noses
Out at Regent's Park Zoo.

        — James Norman Hall

NO MAN'S LAND

No Man's Land is an eerie sight
At early dawn in the pale gray light.
Never a house and never a hedge
In No Man's Land from edge to edge,
And never a living soul walks there
To taste the fresh of the morning air.
Only some lumps of rotting clay,
That were friends or foemen yesterday.

What are the bounds of No Man's Land?
You can see them clearly on either hand,
A mound of rag-bags gray in the sun,
Or a furrow of brown where the earthworks
    run
From the eastern hills to the western sea,
Through field or forest o'er river and lea;
No man may pass them, but aim you well
And Death rides across on the bullet or shell.

But No Man's Land is a goblin sight
When patrols crawl over at dead o' night;
Boche or British, Belgian or French,
You dice with death when you cross the trench.
When the " rapid," like fireflies in the dark,
Flits down the parapet spark by spark,
And you drop for cover to keep your head
With your face on the breast of the four
    months' dead.

The man who ranges in No Man's Land
Is dogged by the shadows on either hand
When the star-shell's flare, as it bursts o'erhead,
Scares the great gray rats that feed on the dead,
And the bursting bomb or the bayonet-snatch
May answer the click of your safety-catch.
For the lone patrol, with his life in his hand,
Is hunting for blood in No Man's Land.

—J. KNIGHT-ADKIN

IN SERVICE

Say, Pa!   What is a service flag?
   I see them everywhere.
There's little stars sewed on them;
   What are they doing there?
Sometimes there's lots of little stars,
   And sometimes just a few,
Poor Widow Jones has only one —
   I saw her crying, too.

My darling boy, those little stars,
   Upon a field of white,
Are emblems of our glorious boys
   Enrolling for the right.
The border, as you see, is red,
   Which represents their blood;
The stars are blue, the heavenly hue;
   The white is always good.
Each star you see means some brave boy
   Has left his hearth and home
And gone to fight for Freedom's cause
   Wherever he may roam.

So when you see a lot of stars
   Lift up your heart with joy,
And when you see a single one,
   Pray for some mother's boy.
They go away, those gallant lads,

Across the wreck-strewn sea;
They go to pledge their country's faith
For God and liberty.
The Stars and Stripes they bear aloft
To join the British flag,
And with the colors of brave France,
They mean to end " Der Tag."
And soon, my boy, that service flag,
Born in the Nation's heart,
Will show the world that, when unfurled,
We proudly take our part.
— J. E. EVANS

THE AMERICAN
By permission of the author

The first long swells of a rising storm ran endlessly past Land's End from the open ocean, and the Ardmore rolled heavily as she headed for the Atlantic. Sea after sea smashed against the blunt bow of the freighter, breaking into stinging clouds of spray that showered over the gun on the forecastle and drove aft, forcing the lookouts to turn their faces from the biting gusts. High on the foremast the man in the crow's-nest protected himself as best he could by crouching low behind his canvas weather-cloth, sliding lower still as each whirling cloud of spray, whistling up from the blunt bow far below, spattered against the swaying mast, to drip in slanting streams back to the deck. Forward of the bridge the seas piled over the weather rail, to rush and gurgle around the hatches and finally to pour in little cascades back into the sea.

In the overheated galley the cook was lashing a pot of stew on to the stove, to prevent its sliding to the heaving deck. He had carefully made it fast, adjusting it to the already well-filled space, when a seaman, bundled up in dripping oilskins, burst in through the door, accompanied by part of a spent wave that spread over the galley floor in a slippery flood.   Following the example of one of his own pots, which at that moment boiled over onto the red-hot stove, the cook turned upon the intruder, sputtering a volley of abuse.

"Aw, come on, Al," replied the seaman. "I didn't mean to let the English Channel in. Give us a cup of coffee.   I'm just off watch."

Al forgot his wrath as quickly as it had come upon him, and reached for the huge coffee-pot that was wedged securely amid the assemblage of cooking utensils on the heated stove. Swinging it with a practiced hand, he poured a cup of the steaming coffee, as he balanced himself to the rolling of the ship, and with a good-natured grin handed it to the waiting sailor.

"I'm glad I ain't on deck to-day," Al said, as he watched the coffee disappear. "Bein' cook ain't just the job for a man, but it's more comfortable than standin' watch and watch in the English Channel in February."

"Well," replied the other, "I won't kick, 'cause the worse job on this ship ain't standin' watch on the bridge.   To my notion, bein' one of them armed guards is the worst.   You ought to see 'em up on the forecastle tryin' to keep from bein' washed overboard and tryin' at the same time to find a sub to shoot at."

The cook looked up and grinned.

"Could they get one a day like this?" he asked.

"They say they could," answered the sailor. "Heavy weather don't seem to make much difference to —"

He stopped abruptly, stood listening for a moment, and jumped for the door. Peering forward through the driving spray, he saw the breech of the forward gun open and an empty shell, still smoking from the discharge, jumped onto the wet deck. The loader, timing his action to the pitch of the ship, slid another shell into the opening, and the plugman slammed home the breech.

The muzzle lifted as the ship rolled and a blinding flash burst from it. A roar rolled down the deck toward the sailor and the cook, both of whom stood clutching the rail, heedless of the breaking seas. Looking intently into the haze, they saw a splash in the tumbling water, and saw, too, the streaming deck of a submarine. The gun on the stern of the Ardmore roared, and another splash appeared beside the submarine. The gun crew forward, working with a precision gained from many a drill, loaded again. The ship slid over a swell, rolling slowly. The pointer elevated the muzzle, and an ear-splitting blast burst forth.

The submarine shuddered beneath the shock. A part of her deck flew into the air, and a sea, driving against her side, buckled her broken back. She pitched laboriously in the heavy seaway as the inrushing water sucked her slowly beneath the surface, while the endless seas surged relentlessly on, playfully tossing two tiny, struggling forms.

Slowly the Ardmore turned and headed toward the spot. On the wing of the bridge a sailor stood, swinging a life-buoy. As the ship passed the struggling men he tossed it into the water. Another life-buoy, thrown by the captain, dropped beside it, and a few minutes later the almost lifeless bodies of two German sailors were dragged over the rail.

" Take them to the galley," ordered the captain, " where it's warm. Al can bring them around."

The two men were presently deposited on the galley floor by the sailors who had hauled them over the side. For a moment the rescuers stood gazing at the dripping forms, until Al, assuming command in his realm of pots and pans, ordered them out so as to allow him to attend to the wants of the unconscious Germans.

The sailors departed, and Al turned to the two bedraggled forms that lay huddled near the stove. He had hardly decided on a course to pursue, however, when one of them opened his eyes.

" Hello," said Al. " How you feelin'? "

The man looked blankly at the cook.

" Oh," continued Al, " you're German; that's right. Well," and he continued in the language of the Fatherland, " so am I. Or at least I was until I went to America. But now I'm an American."

The expression on the face of the German sailor changed.

" American, are you? " he replied. " And you were born in Germany? "

" Yes," answered Al. " Born in Germany and trained in the German army. And I have a brother in the German navy, too."

The other grunted his contempt. Al reached for the pot and poured out a steaming mug of coffee.

" Yes," he continued. " I've been in America six years now, and I've got to where I can see what's wrong with Germany. I used to cheer for the Kaiser, and I thought, just as you do, that he is a sort of superior being. I used to think that the little impudent officers that strutted around were better than I was. I had been trained to think so, and they had been trained to think so, too. So when I was in the army I imagined that they were really better — that their blood was of a different grade, I suppose.

" And then I got out of the army and went to America on a freight ship. When I went ashore in New York, I had a job offered me, and I didn't go back to the ship. And now I'm glad I didn't. I've saved nearly two thousand dollars, being cook in a restaurant. And then this war came on, and they needed more men for the new ships they were building. So I offered to go as cook. I told them that I was born in Germany, but that I wanted to help the world get rid of the Kaiser. I had some trouble getting a ship, but at last our captain took me. This is my second trip over. And we haven't been sunk yet. Instead of that we got you to-day."

He stopped a moment and then continued.

" Why, if you knew what America is you'd want to be an American too."

He seized the coffee-pot again and refilled the sailor's cup.

" Here," he said, " have some more."

He poured out another cupful and turned to the form that still lay quietly on the deck. Seizing the unconscious man, he straightened him up and started to pour the coffee down his throat. He turned the white face toward the light and stifled a cry. The cup clattered from his hand and rolled to and fro about the deck with the rolling of the ship, finally stopping in a dark-red blot that marked the place where the unconscious sailor had been lying.

"Hans!" screamed the cook, as he held the limp form and felt a sticky warmth against his hand where it pressed the sailor's side.

Slowly the wounded man's eyes opened. For a moment he looked blankly at the frightened cook, and then a smile of recognition spread over his face.

"Albert," he said huskily. His eyes rolled aimlessly for a moment, and his head dropped forward. A shudder passed through him, and he collapsed in his brother's arms.

The cook lowered the still form to the deck. He rose to his feet and stood holding unsteadily to the lashing he had put on the pot of stew. The German sailor watched him intently.

"Your brother?" he asked.

The cook nodded slowly, and looked blankly at the form that now moved only with the rolling of the ship. A look of triumph crept into the eyes of the sailor.

"You're no American," he said, and with narrowed eyes watched for the effect of his words. "An American gun just killed your brother."

Al gazed uncomprehendingly at his companion.

"Listen," continued the sailor. "We can get into the hold and open the sea-cocks."

Al set his teeth and stood rigidly as the ship rolled. The German sailor continued.

"We can open the sea-cocks," he repeated. "The ship'll sink. We can get away. We'll be picked up. Come." He rose to his feet and stood waiting for the cook's decision.

Al pulled himself together with the strength of a sudden determination. He looked at the stiffening body of his brother, then glanced up at the sailor.

"Yes, come," he answered, slowly.

Together they stepped out onto the deserted deck, and the sailor's eyes twinkled with devilish glee at winning the American over.

"This way," said the cook, and he led the sailor forward and down a hatchway. He turned and entered a door. The sailor followed, peering around to see that they were not followed.

The captain looked up from a report he was writing.

"I brought this man around," said the cook, slowly. "But the other,"— his voice broke — "my brother — is dead."

— HAWTHORNE DANIEL

CONSOLATION

In summer we suffered from dust and from
    flies,
The flies in our rations, the dust in our eyes,
An' some of our fellows, they dropt in the 'eat,
But the Boche, oh, the Boche, was perspirin'—
    a treat!

There were times when we longed for a tankard
    o' beer,
Bein' sick of warm water — our tipple out 'ere,
But our tongues might be furry an' throats like
    a flue,
Yet it's nothing to wot the fat Boches went
    through.

Now the winter is 'ere with the wet an' the cold,
An' our rifles an' kit are a sight to be'old,
An' in trenches that's flooded we tumble and
    splosh,
" Wot cheer? " we remarks. " It's the same
    for the Boche."

If we're standin' in two foot o' water, you see,
Quite likely the Boches are standin' in three;
An' though the keen frost may be ticklin' our
    toes,
Oo doubts that the Boches' 'ole bodies is froze?

Are we sleepy or sick or 'arf dead for a meal?
Just think of 'ow underfed Boches must feel!
Are we badly in need of a shave an' a wash?
Consider the 'orrible state of a Boche!

So 'ere's philosophy simple and plain,
Wotever we 'ates in the bloomin' campaign,
'Tis balm to our souls, as we grumble and cuss,
To feel that the Boches are 'atin it wuss.

OFF DUTY

The night is full of magic, and the moonlit dew-
  drops glisten
Where the blossoms close in slumber and the
  questing bullets pass —
Where the bullets hit the level I can hear them
  as I listen,
Like a little cricket concert, chirping chorus in
  the grass.

In the dug-out by the traverse there's a candle-
  flame a-winking
And the fireflies on the sandbags have their
  torches all aflame.
As I watch them in the moonlight, sure, I can-
  not keep from thinking,
That the world I knew and this one carry on
  the very same.

Look! A gun flash to the eastward!
  " Cover, matey!   Under cover!
Don't you know the flash of danger? You
  should know that signal well;
You can hear it as it's coming. There it
  passes; swooping over.
There's a threat of desolation in the passing of
  a shell."

Little spears of grass are waving, decked with
jewels iridescent —

Hark! A man on watch is stricken — I can
hear his dying moan —

Lies a road across the starland near the wan
and waning crescent,

Where a sentinel off-duty goes to reach his
Maker's Throne.

— PATRICK MACGILL

LITTLE MOTHER

Permission of the Publishers, The Stewart & Kidd Co.,
Cincinnati

Little mother, little mother, with the shadows
    in your eyes,
    And the icy hand of Fear about your heart,
You cannot help your boy prepare to make his
    sacrifice,
    Unless you make yours bravely at the start!

He is training, as a million others train;
    He is giving what the others give — their
        best;
Make him feel your faith in him, though your
        troubled eyes grow dim;
    Let him know that you can stand the acid
        test!

Because he's joined the colors — he's not dead!
    Because he's found his duty, he's not lost!
Through your mother-love, my dear, keep him
        steady, keep him near,
    To the soul he loves — your soul — what-
        e'er the cost!

You aren't alone in heartaches or in doubts;
    All mothers feel this burden, newly coined;

Then call your trembling pride to your colors
    — to your side —
  "Be a sport!" and make him glad that he
    has joined!

Little mother, little mother, with the shadows
    in your eyes,
  And the icy hand of Fear about your heart,
There is this that you can do: "Play the
    game," there honor lies,
  Now your boy and country need you — do
    your part!
                — EVERARD JACK APPLETON

THE MOTHER ON THE SIDEWALK

By permission of the author and the publishers, Reilly &
Britton, Chicago

The mother on the sidewalk as the troops are
marching by
Is the mother of Old Glory that is waving in
the sky.
Men have fought to keep it splendid, men have
died to keep it bright,
But that flag was born of woman and her suf-
ferings day and night;
'Tis her sacrifice has made it, and once more
we ought to pray
For the brave and loyal mother of the boys that
go away.
There are days of grief before her, there are
hours that she will weep,
There are nights of anxious waiting when her
fears will banish sleep;
She has heard her country calling and has risen
to the test,
She has placed upon the altar of the nation's
need her best.
And no man shall ever suffer in the turmoil of
the fray
The anguish of the mother of the boy who goes
away.

You may boast men's deeds of glory, you may
    tell their courage great,
But to die is easier service than alone to sit and
    wait.
And I hail the little mother, with the tear
    stained face and grave
Who has given the Flag a soldier — she the
    bravest of the brave.
And that banner we are proud of, with its red
    and blue and white,
Is a lasting tribute holy to all mothers' love of
    right.

— EDGAR A. GUEST

SINCE YOU WENT AWAY

Since you went away, every gay sailor lad,
    Every khaki-clad soldier I see,
Has a place in my heart, and a share in my
      thoughts
    And belongs, just a little, to me.
He's a comrade of yours, and is bearing his
      share
    Of the burden that rests upon you;
Both are doing the work that a nation has set
    For its glorious manhood to do.

Since you went away, I have entered within
    A sisterhood — mystic and great —
Of women who've learned the great lesson, to
      give
    And are learning another, to wait.
But I strive, like the rest, not to doubt or to
      fear;
    To murmur, or sigh, or complain,
But to trust in His might, and to know, by His
      grace,
    That your sacrifice cannot be vain.

Since you went away, every fold of the flag
    Has a message that's tender and true;
It has always meant liberty, freedom, and
    right;

It now means my country — and you.
Your honor is part of the deep azure field,
   Your courage of each crimson bar,
And the soul of you, shining, resplendent and
      clear,
   Is a part of each beautiful star.

— ALLISON BROWN

MARCHING AWAY

There is a shrill of bugles,
    There is a sound of drums,
And down the wide and sun-lit street
    A stately column comes
In answer to the bugles' call,
    And to the call of drums.

The sons of loving households,
    Bright youths from shop and store
Who leave their own familiar work,
    For tasks untried before,
They go with sturdy feet and hands,
    And study war's grim lore.

Our smiles and tears are mingled;
    " Dear God, be kind," we pray;
" Be good to these our bonny lads
    Who enter in the fray;
No care of ours can be their shield,
    They go so far away."

Our sons were kindly gentlemen,
    They were not taught to slay,
But, bred to ways of law and peace,
    They saw their life's bright day
Unfolding fair before their eyes,
    With joys of work and play.

But sudden, swift, the bugles' cry
   And drum-beats fill their ears;
They make no protest at the call,
   And trample down their fears,
And we — we watch them march away
   And smile against our tears!

                — EMMA A. E. LENTE

THE PRAYER

Permission of the publishers, Geo. H. Doran Co.,
New York

You say there's only evil in this war —
That bullets drive out Christ? If you had
    been
In Furnes with me that night . . . what would
    you say,
I wonder?
        It was ruin past all words,
Horror where joyous comfort used to be,
And not clean quiet death, for all day long
The great shells tore the little that remained
Like vultures on a body that still breathes.
They stopped as it grew dark. I looked about
The ghastly wilderness that once had been
The village street, and saw no other life
Except a Belgian soldier, shadowy
Among the shadows, and a little group
Of children creeping from a cellar school
And hurrying home. One older than **the**
    rest —
So little older! — mothered them along
Till all at once a stray belated shell
Whined suddenly out of the gloom, and burst
Near by. The babies wailed and clung to-
    gether,
Helpless with fear. In vain the little mother
Encouraged them —" But no! you mustn't cry,

That isn't brave, that isn't French!"   At last
She led her frightened brood across the way
To where there stood a roadside Calvary
Bearing its sad indomitable Christ —
Strange how the shells will spare just that!   I
        saw
So many . . . There they knelt, poor inno-
        cents,
Hands folded and eyes closed.   I stole across
And stood behind them.   "We must say our
        prayer —
Our Father which art in heaven," she began,
And all the little sobbing voices piped,
"Hallowed be Thy Name."   From down the
        road
The Belgian soldier had come near.   I felt
Him standing there beside me in the dusk.
"Thy kingdom come —
                            "Thy will be done on earth
As it is in heaven."   The irony of it
Cut me like steel.   I barely kept an oath
Behind my teeth.   If one could name this earth
In the same breath with heaven — what is hell?
Only a little child could pray like this.
"Give us this day our daily bread —"   A
        pause.
There was no answer.   She repeated it
Urgently.   Still the hush.   She opened wide

Reproachful eyes at them.   Their eyes were
   open
Also, and staring at the shadowy shapes
Of ruin all around them.   Now that prayer
Had grown too hard even for little children.
" I know — I know — but we must say the
   prayer,"
She faltered.   " Give us this day our daily
   bread,
And — and forgive —" she stopped.
                          " Our trespasses
As we forgive them who have trespassed
   against us."
The children turned amazed to see who spoke
The words they could not.   I too turned to
   him,
The soldier there beside me — and I looked
Into King Albert's face . . . I have no words
To tell you what I saw . . . only I thought
That while a man's breast held a heart like
   that,
Christ was not — even here — so far away.
                    — AMELIA JOSEPHINE BURR

ON ACTIVE SERVICE

For the bloke on Active Service, w'en 'e goes
    across the sea,
'E's sure to stand in terror of the things 'e
    doesn't see,
A 'and grenade or mortar as it leaves the other
    side
You can see an' 'ear it comin', so you simply
    steps aside.
The aeroplane above you may go droppin'
    bombs a bit,
But lyin' in your dug-out you're unlucky if
    you're 'it.
We'n the breezes fills your trenches with has-
    fixiatin' gas,
You puts on your respirator an' allows the stuff
    to pass.
W'n you're up against a feller with a bayonet
    long an' keen,
Just 'ave purchase of your weapon an' you'll
    drill the beggar clean.
W'n man and 'oss is chargin' you, upon your
    knees you kneel,
An' catch the 'oss's breastbone with an inch or
    two of steel.
It's sure to end its canter, an' as the creature
    stops

The rider pitches forward, an' you catch 'im as
'e drops.
It's w'en 'e sees 'is danger, an' 'e knows 'is way
about
That a bloke is blamed lucky if 'e's knocked
completely out.
But out on Active Service there are dangers
everywhere,
The shrapnel shell and bullet that comes on you
unaware,
The saucy little rifle is a perky little maid,
An' w'en you've got 'er message you 'ave done
your last parade.
The four-point-five will seek you from some dis-
tant leafy wood,
An' taps you on the napper an' you're out of
step for good.
From the gun within the spinney to a sniper up
a tree
There are terrors waitin' Tommy in the things
'e doesn't see.

— PATRICK MacGILL

THE AMERICANS COME!

Permission of *Munsey's Magazine,* New York

" What is the cheering, my little one?
    Oh, that my blinded eyes could see!
Hasten, my boy, to the window run,
    And see what the noise in the street may be.

" I hear the drums and the marching feet;
    Look and see what it's all about!
Who can it be that our people greet
      With cheers and laughter and joyous
        shout? "

" There are men, my father, brown and strong,
    And they carry a banner of wondrous hue;
With a mighty tread they swing along;
    Now I see white stars on a field of blue! "

" You say that you see white stars on blue?
    Look, are there stripes of red and white?
It must be — yes, it must be true!
    Oh, dear God, if I had my sight!

" Hasten, son, fling the window wide;
    Let me kiss the staff our flag swings from
And salute the Stars and Stripes with pride,
    For, God be praised, the Americans come! "
              — ELIZABETH A. WILBUR

TO A CANADIAN AVIATOR WHO DIED FOR HIS COUNTRY IN FRANCE

Permission of the author and *Scribner's Magazine,*
New York

Tossed like a falcon from the hunter's wrist,
A sweeping plunge, a sudden shattering noise,
And thou hast dared with a long spiral twist
The elastic stairway to the rising sun.
Peril below thee and above, peril
Within thy car; but peril cannot daunt
Thy peerless heart: gathering wing and poise,
Thy plane transfigured, and thy motor-chant
Subdued to a murmur — then a silence,—
And thou art but a disembodied venture
In the void.

But Death, who has learned to fly,
Still matchless when his work is to be done,
Met thee between the armies and the sun;
Thy speck of shadow faltered in the sky;
Then thy dead engine and thy broken wings
Drooped through the arc and passed in fire,—
A wreath of smoke — a breathless exhalation.
But ere that vision sealed thine eyes,
Lulling thy senses with oblivion;
And from its sliding station in the skies
Thy dauntless soul upward in circles soared

To the sublime and purest radiance whence it
    sprang.

In all their eyries eagles shall mourn thy fate,
And leaving on the lonely crags and scaurs
Their unprotected young, shall congregate
High in the tenuous heaven and anger the sun
With screams, and with a wild audacity
Dare all the battle danger of thy flight;
Till weary with combat one shall desert the
    light,
Fall like a bolt of thunder and check his fall
On the high ledge, smoky with mist and cloud,
Where his neglected eaglets shriek aloud,
And drawing the film across his sovereign sight
Shall dream of thy swift soul immortal
Mounting in circles, faithful beyond death.
               — DUNCAN CAMPBELL SCOTT

AMERICA GOES IN SINGING

" The American troops will fight side by side with the British and French troops and the Star Spangled Banner will float beside the French and English flags in the plains of Picardy."

This was the official answer to General Pershing's words to General Foch:

" All that we have are yours, to dispose of them as you will."

When Pershing stood at the tomb of Lafayette and uttered the briefest and finest war address that has been delivered, " Lafayette, we are here! " he spoke for the American spirit, to the soul of the French people. Our country from sea to sea ratified the message of a soldier unafraid. It was

> " The voice of one for millions,
> In whom the millions rejoice
> For giving their one spirit voice."

Even so with Pershing's offer of our whole armed force at once, to beat back the tidal wave of the flagellated myrmidons of Prussia. The country that we love will send into No Man's Land, to reclaim it for God and from the Devil, its first hundred thousand, its million, and then its millions more, if they are needed, to assure the triumph of the right and the salvation of the world from the glutted maw of the Beast of Beasts, of Moloch in a death's-head helmet.

Our men, our sons and brothers, march on singing toward the fray. The Irish poet Arthur O'Shaughnessy has told us that

> " Three with a new song's measure
> Can trample an empire down."

Terrible indeed is the striking power of a singing army — as Cromwell's psalm-singing Ironsides proved. Mile after mile of men in khaki, tramping the measured cadence down the miry highways to the front, are lifting in lyric unison their battle anthems —" Where Do We Go From Here, Boys? " and " Over There " and " Pack Up Your Troubles in Your Old Kit Bag." These swarming caravans moving toward the firing line like inspired clockwork, without confusion — these rumbling guns outlandishly bespotted to hide them from the prying eyes aloft — these motor-trucks and rocking, rumbling wagons roofed with brown, and above all and before all, these marching columns of men pressing forward to relieve the warworn thousands in the trenches with their irrepressible youth and strength and high, joking courage — all this means for us at home and for us who are over there a shining dream brought true, a great day dawning for America, a saving grace for our country where liberty, so dearly bought by the blood of our fathers, is forever cherished and forever sanctified.

America is in the fight because she " can do no other." Our men could not endure to wait an hour longer. "Watchman, what of the night?" was the interrogation that ran from armed camp to armed camp. Their brothers beneath the Union Jack and the Tricolor were in the thick of the hardest battle ever waged on earth, and were falling and dying. With a righteous indignation burning in their heart, and on their lips the song of the happy warrior who vindicates the right, our men march forward into battle — their faces to the enemy — their love with us at home — their glory safe with God.

— *Public Ledger,* Philadelphia

THE KID HAS GONE TO THE COLORS

By permission of the author

The Kid has gone to the Colors,
　And we don't know what to say;
The Kid we have loved and cuddled
　Stepped out for the flag to-day.
We thought him a child, a baby,
　With never a care at all;
But his country called him man-size —
　And the Kid has heard the call.

He paused to watch the recruiting,
　Where, fired by the fife and drum,
He bowed his head to Old Glory,
　And thought that it whispered " Come! "
The Kid not being a slacker,
　Stood forth with patriot-joy
To add his name to the roster
　And, God! we're proud of the boy!

The Kid has gone to the Colors;
　It seems but a little while
Since he drilled a schoolboy army
　In a truly martial style.
But now he's a man, a soldier,
　And we lend him a listening ear;
For his heart is a heart all loyal,
　Unscourged by the curse of fear.

His dad, when he told him, shuddered;
　　His mother — God bless her! — cried;
Yet, blest with a mother-nature
　　She wept with a mother-pride.
But he whose old shoulders straightened
　　Was granddad — for memory ran
To years when he, too, a youngster,
　　Was changed by the Flag to a man!
　　　　　　　　　— WILLIAM HERSCHELL

RHEIMS

It was a people's church — stout, plain folk
    they,
Wanting their own cathedral, not the king's,
Nor prelate's, nor great noble's.   On the walls,
On porch and arch and doorway — see — the
    saints
Have the plain people's faces.   That sweet
    Virgin
Was young Marie, who lived around the
    corner,
And whom the sculptor knew.   From time to
    time
He saw her at her work or with her babe,
So gay, so dainty, smiling at the child.
That sturdy Peter — Peter of the keys —
He was old Jean, the Breton fisherman,
Who, somehow, made his way here from the
    coast
And lived here many years, yet kept withal
The look of the great sea and his great nets.
And John there, the beloved, was Etienne,
And good Saint James was François —
    brothers they,
And had a small, clean bakeshop, where they
    sold
Bread, cakes, and little pies.   Well, so it went!

These were not Italy's saints, nor yet the gods,
Majestic, calm, unmoved, of ancient Greece.
No, they were only townsfolk, common people,
And graced a common church — that stood and
    stood
Through war and fire and pestilence, through
    ravage
Of time and kings and conquerors, till at last
The century dawned which promised common
    men
The things they long had hoped for!
                     O the time
Showed a fair face, was daughter of great
    Demos,
Flamboyant, bore a light, laughed loud and
    free,
And feared not any man — until — until —
There sprang a mailed figure from a throne,
Gorgeous, imperial, glowing — a monstrosity
Magnificent as death and as death terrible.
It walked these aisles and saw the humble ones,
Peter, the fisherman, James and John the shop-
    keepers,
And Mary, sweet, gay, innocent and poor.
Loud did it laugh and long. "These peaceful
    folk!
What place have they in my great armed
    world?"

Then with its thunderbolts of fire it drove
These saints from out their places — breaking
    roof,
Wall, window, portal — and the great grave
    arch
Smoked with the awful funeral smoke of doom.

Thus died they and their church — but from
    the wreck
Of fire and smoke and broken wood and stone
There rose a figure greater far than they —
Their Lord who dwells within no house of
    hands;
Whose beauty hath no need of any form!
Out from the fire he passed, and round him
    went
Marie and Jean, and Etienne and François,
And they went singing, singing, through their
    France —
And Italy — and England — and the world!
        — Margaret Steele Anderson

MATEY

(Cambrin, May, 1915)

Not comin' back to-night, matey,
And reliefs are comin' through,
We're all goin' out all right, matey,
Only we're leavin' you.
Gawd! it's a bloody sin, matey,
Now that we've finished the fight,
We go when reliefs come in, matey,
But you're stayin' 'ere to-night.

Over the top is cold, matey —
You lie on the field alone,
Didn't I love you of old, matey,
Dearer than the blood of my own?
You were my dearest chum, matey —
(Gawd! but your face is white)
But now, though reliefs 'ave come, matey,
I'm goin' alone to-night.

I'd sooner the bullet was mine, matey —
Goin' out on my own,
Leavin' you 'ere in the line, matey,
All by yourself, alone.
Chum o' mine and you're dead, matey,
And this is the way we part,
The bullet went through your head, matey,
But Gawd! it went through my 'eart.

      — Patrick MacGill

THE OHIO MEN

Ohio of the grassland and the waving, billowy
　　plain,
Ohio of the rolling hills cloaked in the golden
　　grain;
Ohio, whose pure beauty now needs no poet's
　　pen —
Ohio sends to fight for God, her brave Ohio
　　men.

They are marching, marching, marching from
　　the grassland and the wheat,
And down the cities, clicking, goes the tramp of
　　myriad feet;
Men are marching, marching, marching, for
　　the good old State again —
God bless them and God keep them, the good
　　Ohio men!

Men march from out Ohio as they marched
　　from her before,
To lay their good lives down for God out there
　　at Freedom's war,
To lay their yesterdays away and all that's
　　sweetly been;
And let us not forget them now, the good Ohio
　　men!

Their mother, Great America, now calls her
    sons to fight,
And from Ohio comes the bugle like a cry from
    out the night;
They are loyal, they are heroes, and they need
    no poet's pen —
God bless them and protect them now, the
    brave Ohio men!

While all the world is bleeding, they will bear
    the torch of light;
They will battle now for Liberty, for Justice,
    and for Right.
And the old, old blood of heroes caught in the
    young, young sod
Goes marching off across the world to fight for
    Peace and God.

They are marching, marching, marching from
    the grassland and the wheat,
And down the cities, clicking, goes the tramp of
    myriad feet;
Men are marching, marching, marching from
    the good old State again —
God bless them and God keep them, the brave
    Ohio men!

— EDWIN CURRAN

A CAROL FROM FLANDERS

In Flanders on the Christmas morn
　　The trenchèd foemen lay,
The German and the Briton born —
　　And it was Christmas day.

The red sun rose on fields accurst,
　　The gray fog fled away;
But neither cared to fire the first,
　　For it was Christmas day.

They called from each to each across
　　The hideous disarray
(For terrible had been their loss) :
　　" Oh, this is Christmas day ! "

Their rifles all they set aside,
　　One impulse to obey;
'Twas just the men on either side,
　　Just men — and Christmas day.

They dug the graves for all their dead
　　And over them did pray;
And Englishman and German said:
　　" How strange a Christmas day ! "

Between the trenches they did meet
　　Shook hands, and e'en did play

At games on which their hearts are set
  On happy Christmas day.

Not all the Emperors and Kings,
  Financiers, and they
Who rule us could prevent these things —
  For it was Christmas day.

O ye who read this truthful rime
  From Flanders, kneel and say:
God speed the time when every day
  Shall be as Christmas day.

— FREDERICK NIVEN

THE RIDERS

There is a rumbling in the graves
   All up and down the land.
There is a lifting of the graves
   And a murmur on every hand.
A murmur in the green grass,
   A stirring in the mound,
A gasping and a questioning,
A shouting and a challenging,
A calling of voices, voices, voices,
   Out of the sacred ground.

There is a stirring in the graves
   All up and down the land.
And a rising of ghostly shapes
From the hillside and the seaside,
   From the red loam and the sand.
Old men, young men, brave men and strong!
   Old men, young men, with anger on their
      lips!
Men who perished moaning, and men who died
      with a song,
   On the hillcrest and the ryefield and the decks
      of battered ships!

Up from the fields of Valley Forge,
   Ghosts and ghosts and ghosts!
Up from the hills of Gettysburg,

Hosts and hosts and hosts!
Old men, young men, out of the earth they
    rise,
  Defenders, defenders!
With their spirits in their eyes!
The ghosts are not an army
  With sword and gleaming gun.
They are riders like the rider
  Who rode to Lexington.
Hark! The hoofs in the night,
And the cry, Awake!
What shapes in the dark?
Hark!
Again, Awake!
Ghosts are riding!
What fingers shake
The doors, and rattle
The windows?
Awake!
Battle!
Riders, riders,
On plain and steep!
Awake, oh, ye that sleep!
Awake, Maine!
Stir from your slumber, Alabama!
Awake from dreams of ease,
Glittering coasts!
Awake, Wisconsin!
On your highways

Are ghosts!
Texas, bestir your sons!
Oregon, make haste!
Riders!
Our dead have arisen!
From graves have they sprung up!
From the hills,
From the shores,
They come, the valiant,
And knock at our doors!
Ghosts of our fathers!
Dismayed!
That we they died for
Should tremble, should bluster,
Should falter,
Be afraid!
What hoof-beats, Montana?
Illinois, what cries?
Up from your battle-graves,
Virginia, they rise!
What eyes light the darkness?
What voices command?
Mark them, Mississippi!
Be glad for them, Rio Grande!
Leap up from your beds
When they come, New England!
Hark!   Down the misty valley —
Awake!
Nearer!   Hoof-beats!

Awake!
Meet on the Common!
The world's at stake!

On the highways they ride, our fathers!
   They knock at our doors in the night!
Have you no ear for Justice?
   Have you no hands for the Right?
Up from your beds, you dawdlers!
   Say not we died in vain.
Out of the rusty scabbard
   Whip the spirit again!

The ghosts are not an army
   With sword and gleaming gun.
They are riders like the rider
   Who rode to Lexington!
And every sash they rattle,
   And every door they shake;
And to every goal-forgetful soul
To every slumbering, laggard soul,
   They cry, Craven, awake!
            — HERMAN HAGEDORN

THE CONVERSATION BOOK

I 'ave a conversation book: I brought it out
    from 'ome,
It tells the French for knife and fork, an' like-
    wise brush and comb;
It learns you 'ow to ast the time, the names of
    all the stars,
An' 'ow to order oysters an' 'ow to buy cigars.

But there ain't no shops to shop in, there ain't
    no grand hotels,
When you spend your days in dugouts doin'
    'olesale trade in shells;
It's nice to know the proper talk for theaters
    an' such —
But when it comes to talkin', why, it doesn't
    'elp you much.

There's all them friendy kind o' things you'd
    naturally say,
When you meet a fellow casual-like an' pass the
    time o' day —
Them little things as breaks the ice an' kind o'
    clears the air,
Which, when you turn the phrase book up, why,
    them things isn't there!

I met a chap the other day a-roostin' in a trench,
'E didn't know a word of ours nor me a word o'
    French;

An' 'ow it was we managed, well, I cannot
    understand,
But I never used the phrase book though I 'ad
    it in my 'and.

I winked at 'im to start with; 'e grinned from
    ear to ear;
An' 'e says " Tipperary " an' I says " Sou-
    venir,"
'E 'ad my only Woodbine, I 'ad 'is thin cigar,
Which set the ball a'rollin', an' so — well, there
    you are!

I showed 'im next my wife an' kids, 'e up and
    showed me 'is.
Them funny little Frenchy kids with 'air all in
    a fizz;
" Annette," 'e says, " Louise," 'e says, an' 'is
    tears began to fall;
We was comrades when we parted, but we'd
    'ardly spoke at all.

'E'd 'ave kissed me if I'd let 'im; we 'ad never
    met before,
An' I've never seen the beggar since, for that's
    the way o' war;
An' tho we scarcely spoke a word, I wonder
    just the same
If 'e'll ever see them kids of 'is — I never ast
    'is name!

THE SOLDIER'S MOTHER

After all, there is no love like a mother's love.   She loves her unborn babe with a tender, wistful, yearning love which makes the anguish of her sufferings a joy unspeakable.   When the little one is placed in her arms exultant joy fills her heart.   The wee baby rules this mother heart, and the growing child is her first thought in the morning hour and her last prayer as she rests her weary head upon her pillow.   She is generally reticent and undemonstrative, but her boy is the joy of her heart and the gladness of her life.   This wise and loving mother knows her boy must have companionships intimate and dear, and she does not interfere. Her boy becomes a man, and gradually he forms his circle of friendships, and as time goes on he is overwhelmed by the mystery and gladness of a great love.   His mother understands, and with a tender light in her eyes she withdraws herself just a little more.   Then comes the joy and bewilderment of the growing family and new chambers are unlocked in her " boy's " heart, but the mother, now growing old, understands, and there is no jealousy in her heart.

She sits alone much these days, but her memory is busy, and her heart holds a secret of that love which began before her boy was born — that boy who is now a great man with a home and babies of his own. How sweet and holy and God-like is mother's love!

In the great and devastating war no one can ever estimate the suffering of the mothers of all lands. With complete self-forgetfulness they have said farewell to their boys. The women of Sparta were not braver than the women of the warring countries of to-day. And now our American mothers must lay their sons on the altar of their country, and they will do so with a heroism unsurpassed by the mothers of any country or any generation. Others will suffer, but the suffering of our mothers will be as sweet and holy and God-like as their love.

If it pleases God, many of our noble young men will come unscathed through the dragon-guarded gates of war. Flushed with victory, decorated with badges of honor, grown strong with burden-bearing, these boys will come home amid the plaudits and tears of welcome hosts. Mother, may your boy be among those who will thus come home! But if not, you will remember that it will be his glory to die for his beloved country. You will rejoice that he went forward with undaunted mien and unflinching eye, and that, like Nathan Hale, he was sorry that he had but one life to lose for his country!   *Watchman Examiner*

IN PRAISE OF RIGHTEOUS WAR

I am coming not in a weakling's verse, with a
    milksop's feeble whine,
With uplifted hand and with soft-voiced drawl,
    aghast at the battle-line;
But I come to praise the fight that is fought for
    the sake of Truth and Right,
The fight that is fought for God and for Home,
    that will mate the Right with Might.

Yes, patience is good, and humility, too, and so
    is the pipe of peace;
But the time will come when forbearance ends,
    and your sugary smiles must cease;
Then either your hand must grip at your gun
    and brighten the sword from its rust,
Or your slavish neck must bend to the yoke, and
    your mouth must chew the dust.

You must fight for the fire that toasts your feet,
    for the roof that shelters your head,
For the herd that yields you its milk or meat,
    for the field that gives you bread;
You must fight for bed, you must fight for
    board, for the woman you love the best.
And, oh, you must fight with a tenfold will for
    the baby at her breast.

When a mad dog comes down your village
    street, with the green foam in his jaws,
Do you greet him with Bibles and hymn-books,
    and lovingly bid him pause?
When a rattlesnake rises amidst your path,
    alert with its fiery sting,
Do you pet him, and pat him, and wish him
    well, and a song of welcome sing?

When a big-armed bully among the Powers
    says the folk of a little land
Must sprawl in the dirt and confess to a crime
    that never besmirched their land,
Do you blame that people that rises up a pigmy
    ready to fight,
A David aroused, with only a sling, defying
    Goliath's might?

When a vain war-lord with a swollen head, in-
    flamed with a brute desire,
Through a little State that was lapped in peace
    comes tramping with blood and fire
Despoiling the fields and looting the towns —
    do you blame that blameless state
For rousing in Godlike righteous wrath and
    hitting with righteous hate?

And war is the great Arouser; it silences whim-
    pering tongues;

It toughens the muscles, it hardens the fist, and
    brings fresh air to the lungs;
Though it comes with torch and it strikes with
    steel, and shorten's life's petty span,
That life it exalts to heroic heights, so a man is
    twice a man.

Yes, patience is good, and so is peace; but he is
    not worthy of good,
Who will not rush forth when the spoiler comes
    to defend it with his blood;
When that spoiler comes with his bandit crew to
    shatter with shot and shell,
Let the good man rise, with a fervent prayer,
    and give him hell for hell!
                — WALTER MALONE

YOUR LAD, AND MY LAD

Permission of the author

Down toward the deep-blue water, marching to
throb of drum,
From city street and country lane the lines of
khaki come;
The rumbling guns, the sturdy tread, are full of
grim appeal,
While rays of western sunshine flash back from
burnished steel.
With eager eyes and cheeks aflame the serried
ranks advance;
And your dear lad, and my dear lad, are on
their way to France.

A sob clings choking in the throat, as file on file
sweep by,
Between those cheering multitudes, to where
the great ships lie;
The batteries halt, the columns wheel, to clear-
toned bugle-call,
With shoulders squared and faces front they
stand a khaki wall.
Tears shine on every watcher's cheek, love
speaks in every glance,
For your dear lad, and my dear lad, are on their
way to France.

Between them, through a mist of years, in
    soldier buff or blue,
Brave comrades from a thousand fields watch
    now in proud review;
The same old Flag,— the same old Faith —
    the Freedom of the World —
Spells duty in those flapping folds above long
    ranks unfurled.
Strong are the hearts which bear along Democ-
    racy's advance,
As your dear lad, and my dear lad, go on their
    way to France.

The word rings out; a million feet tramp for-
    ward on the road,
Along that path of sacrifice, o'er which their
    fathers strode.
With eager eyes and cheeks aflame, with cheers
    on smiling lips,
These fightng men of '17 move onward to their
    ships.
Nor even love may hold them back, or halt that
    stern advance,
As your dear lad, and my dear lad, go on their
    way to France.

— RANDALL PARRISH

BOTH WORSHIPED THE SAME
GREAT NAME

Jack Smith belonged to the Y. M. C. A.
   Pat Sheehan to the K. of C.
Both marched away 'neath the flag one day
   To fight for the Land of the Free.
Jack bowed his head as he said a prayer,
   Pat knelt with his parish priest.
Then they stood up square to go " over there "
   To grapple the Hunnish beast.

Now their altar rails were not the same,
   Though they camped in the same old shack.
But just the same 'twas the same Great Name
   They worshiped, both Pat and Jack.
While Jack stood straight as he humbly prayed,
   Pat knelt at a candled shrine;
But the same great God heard each whispered
     word
That harkens to yours and mine.

They didn't agree, did Jack and Pat,
   On methods of worship true;
But what of that? They went to the mat
   For the old Red, White and Blue.
They knelt apart, but 'twas side by side,
   They fought for their homes and right

And the blood-red tide of the kaiser's pride
    They battled by day and night.

Each bullet its billet has got, they say,
    And always will find some mark.
And Pat and Jack in a trench mud black
    Lay side by side in the dark.
Their life's blood ebbed with a failing tide
    As they came toward the Great Unknown;
But hand in hand from that far-off land
    They knew they were not alone.

So " over the top " to the Glory Side,
    Where never is war nor tears;
Where the true and tried in God's love abide
    With nothing of doubts nor fears.
And the God they met as they entered in
    Where the souls of all men are free,
Was the God of Jack's Y. M. C. A.
    And the God of Pat's K. of C.